Improving Water Management

Recent OECD Experience

OECD

ORGANISATION FOR ECONOMIC CO-OPERATION AND DEVELOPMENT

ORGANISATION FOR ECONOMIC CO-OPERATION AND DEVELOPMENT

Pursuant to Article 1 of the Convention signed in Paris on 14th December 1960, and which came into force on 30th September 1961, the Organisation for Economic Co-operation and Development (OECD) shall promote policies designed:

- to achieve the highest sustainable economic growth and employment and a rising standard of living in member countries, while maintaining financial stability, and thus to contribute to the development of the world economy;
- to contribute to sound economic expansion in member as well as non-member countries in the process of economic development; and
- to contribute to the expansion of world trade on a multilateral, non-discriminatory basis in accordance with international obligations.

The original member countries of the OECD are Austria, Belgium, Canada, Denmark, France, Germany, Greece, Iceland, Ireland, Italy, Luxembourg, the Netherlands, Norway, Portugal, Spain, Sweden, Switzerland, Turkey, the United Kingdom and the United States. The following countries became members subsequently through accession at the dates indicated hereafter: Japan (28th April 1964), Finland (28th January 1969), Australia (7th June 1971), New Zealand (29th May 1973), Mexico (18th May 1994), the Czech Republic (21st December 1995), Hungary (7th May 1996), Poland (22nd November 1996), Korea (12th December 1996) and the Slovak Republic (14th December 2000). The Commission of the European Communities takes part in the work of the OECD (Article 13 of the OECD Convention).

Preface

The UN International Year of Freshwater in 2003 will help the international community to focus on how to increase the availability of high-quality water in many parts of the world. An estimated one-fifth of the world's people still do not have access to safe drinking water, and one-third lack adequate sanitation facilities. Many ecosystems are being degraded, deprived of the minimum flows of water on which their ecology depends, as excessive amounts of water are diverted to other uses or become increasingly polluted.

The OECD Environmental Strategy for the First Decade of the 21st Century, adopted by OECD Environment Ministers and endorsed by Ministers of Economics and Finance in 2001, highlights freshwater as a priority for policy action, and articulates two key challenges facing OECD member countries:

- *To manage the use of freshwater resources and associated watersheds so as to maintain adequate supply of freshwater of suitable quality for human use and to support aquatic and other ecosystems.*
- *To protect, restore and prevent deterioration of all bodies of surface water and groundwater to ensure the achievement of water quality objectives in OECD countries.*

As a partial response, most countries have accepted the goal of halving by 2015 the number of people worldwide who do not have access to safe drinking water and sanitation, as agreed in the Millennium Development Goals and at the World Summit on Sustainable Development. These goals will be difficult to meet, especially since we already see a significant gap between the finances needed to meet these goals and the finances that are currently available. And yet these goals do not go far enough; they will still leave more than an estimated half a billion people without access to safe drinking water supplies and over 1 billion without access to adequate sanitation facilities.

Water is a scarce commodity, with competing uses for ecological systems, human health and sanitation, and economic development (e.g. agriculture and industry). Managing this resource well is therefore not an easy task, and must consider all three dimensions of sustainable development – environmental, social, and economic – in an integrated manner.

This report, produced as an input to the Third World Water Forum, brings together the results of various OECD projects on how to manage water resources efficiently and effectively. These draw on extensive experiences in OECD countries with water management and water pricing systems. They also build on lessons learned in OECD work with countries in transition and China (on financing water services infrastructure) and with donor countries (on bilateral and multilateral aid to support water objectives).

The OECD is fully committed to supporting better water management policies, both within its Member countries and through new partnerships with developing and transition economies.

Donald Johnston
Secretary-General of the OECD

Foreword

This report summarises some of the main lessons learned through a range of OECD projects related to the development and implementation of better water management policies. It presents experiences in both OECD and non-OECD (mainly in Eastern Europe, Caucaus and Central Asia and in China) countries. The report is also a key OECD contribution to the Third World Water Forum (Kyoto-Shiga-Osaka, Japan, March 2003).

Following an overview of the main water management challenges, the report addresses the four framework conditions that the OECD has identified as being necessary to support water-related sustainable development:

- Making wider use of markets.
- Improving decision-making processes and institutions for better policy coherence.
- Harnessing science and technology.
- Working with developing countries to address internationally shared objectives.

Each section begins by reviewing that section's relevance to water management in general, with the ensuing chapters focusing on specific OECD work in the area. The report therefore does not provide a comprehensive review of all important water management issues, but rather highlights some of the lessons the OECD has learned during the course of several water-related projects it has carried out in recent years.

The report was prepared by a Task Force in the OECD, including representatives from several OECD Directorates. Lilian Saade-Hazin, Tom Jones, and Helen Mountford within the Environment Directorate were responsible for co-ordinating the work and consolidating the final output. Other main contributors to the drafting included: the Development Co-operation Directorate (Michael Roeskau, Julia Benn, Carol Gabyzon, Valérie Gaveau, Rémy Paris, and Elisabeth Thioleron), the Environment Directorate (Ken Ruffing, Christian Avérous, Brendan Gillespie, Peter Börkey, Nick Johnstone, Kumi Kitamori, and Olga Savran), the Directorate for Food, Agriculture, and Fisheries (Kevin Parris and Makeo Takino) and the Directorate for Science, Technology, and Industry (Elettra Ronchi). Rebecca Brite provided editorial support. The report also benefited from contributions made by the OECD Working Party on Global and Structural Policies. Each of these contributions is gratefully acknowledged.

The report is published under the responsibility of the Secretary-General of the OECD.

Table of Contents

ISBN 92-64-09948-4
Improving Water Management
Recent OECD Experience
© OECD 2003

Executive Summary

*Poor water management poses a serious challenge
to sustainable development worldwide...*

There is widespread concern that poor water management will be one of the major factors limiting sustainable development during the next few decades. Water shortages are common in many regions, and are exacerbated by the pollution or degradation of many water bodies. There are conflicting demands for available water resources, both between human, economic, and ecosystem needs and between regions sharing a single water basin, in some cases leading to geopolitical security threats. World population roughly doubled over the last 50 years, while water consumption worldwide quadrupled. With urban populations growing faster than rural populations, the financial pressures on urban water utilities are intensifying.

*... with significant scarcity in some areas restricting
human use of water resources...*

Securing safe, reliable, reasonably priced water and sanitation services for all is one of the leading challenges facing sustainable development. At the beginning of the 21st century, 1.1 billion people still do not have access to safe water and 2.4 billion lack access to basic sanitation. There are internationally agreed targets to halve these numbers by 2015, set as part of the Millennium Development Goals and the Plan of Implementation of the World Summit on Sustainable Development, respectively.

... and degrading ecosystems.

Meeting these basic human needs is only part of the challenge; increasingly, attention is also focusing on the importance of assuring sufficient water flows in the environment to support essential ecosystem services. In the developing world, 90% of all wastewater still goes untreated into local rivers/streams. An estimated 47 countries (with roughly one-third of the world's population) are classified as suffering medium-high or high water stress. Of these, 17 already extract more water annually than is recharged through their natural water cycles. The increasing pollution of some water bodies further restricts available supplies, and degrades water-dependent ecosystems and the services they provide.

In OECD countries, many surface freshwater bodies still do not meet baseline quality standards, while degradation of groundwater resources appears to be worsening. Pollution of water bodies by farm nutrients and chemicals is an increasing problem, as is contamination by heavy metals and persistent organic pollutants. Subsidies for water use continue to exacerbate problems of over-abstraction and pollution. The lack of adequate financing hampers the maintenance, upgrading, and expansion of water supply and sanitation systems. While access to water services has increased significantly, many OECD countries now face concerns about their affordability.

Despite these problems, some progress is being made.

Despite these negative trends, some progress is being made. For example, OECD countries have significantly reduced industrial and urban discharges to waterways, with the total share of the population connected to public wastewater treatment plants in OECD countries reaching an average of 65% (see figure), and many of the rest using private sewage treatment. OECD countries have also cleaned up a number of the worst polluted freshwater bodies. They have increased their water use efficiency, with several realising overall reductions in water use over the last two decades. Many have started

Sewerage and sewage treatment connection rates in OECD countries (latest year available)

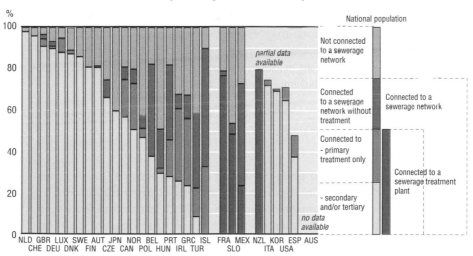

Key Elements of Effective Water Management

Making Markets Work

- Ensure that financial resources are adequate.
- Levy charges that reflect the real marginal costs of water service provision, and thus provide incentives for efficient water use.
- Address any negative social impacts of water pricing policies.

Improving the Coherence of Decision Making

- Apply integrated "whole-basin" and ecosystem approaches.
- Work with the private sector.

Harnessing Science and Technology

- Improve technologies for protecting drinking water quality.
- Improve the efficiency of water use.

Working in Partnership with Developing Countries

- Support international water goals.

to apply more integrated approaches to water management, following a "whole-basin" or "ecosystem" approach.

Important lessons can be drawn from experience…

Some of the main lessons for improved water management that OECD countries have learned through their experiences include: making wider use of markets; improving the coherence of decision making; harnessing science and technology; and working in partnership with developing countries to address internationally shared objectives (see box).

… to help make better use of water pricing mechanisms,…

Water pricing structures and price levels vary greatly among OECD countries due to differences in availability of water resources, in demand, and in institutional and cultural frameworks. In general, OECD countries are moving towards water pricing schedules that reflect the full marginal costs of providing water services, and systems that better target available support to low-income users. These developments help provide incentives for efficient water use and generate funds for necessary infrastructure development and expansion, while assuring affordable water services for all.

... including reform of water subsidy programmes (e.g. in agriculture),...

While pricing structures for municipal and industrial water services increasingly reflect the full costs of providing the services, agricultural water use – primarily for irrigation – remains heavily subsidised, which encourages inefficient use of often scarce resources.

... while addressing any social impacts of water pricing policies,

Concern about the affordability of household water services for vulnerable groups (*e.g.* low-income households and retired people) has led to the development of policy measures aimed at resolving affordability problems while still meeting economic and environmental goals. In general, policies that target specific vulnerable groups – such as through income-related support – have been found to be more efficient at achieving all three objectives than across-the-board subsidies.

Experiences in non-OECD countries illustrate difficulties in funding the maintenance and expansion of water infrastructure.

Recent OECD work has examined water pricing policies in the countries of Eastern Europe, the Caucasus, and Central Asia (EECCA), and in China. Unlike most OECD countries, many of these countries face serious financial deficits in the water sector. This results in under-funding of necessary maintenance and expansion of water and wastewater treatment infrastructure. In the EECCA countries the extensive water infrastructure left from the communist period is deteriorating significantly, resulting in reduced service quality and increased health and environmental risks. These countries face significant problems maintaining the existing infrastructure, let alone expanding it. OECD work with EECCA countries and China is currently focusing on developing realistic plans to finance infrastructure maintenance and expansion through application of water charges, in combination with other available financing.

Coherent decision making requires more integrated water management...

Many OECD countries have significantly changed the institutional and management structures through which their water services are provided. These changes have included a move towards more integrated approaches to water management, including managing resources across the full river basin (*i.e.* using a "whole-basin" or "ecosystem" approach). For most of these countries, comprehensive frameworks of water management laws, policies, programmes, and institutions have been established, and enforcement of water regulations has been strengthened.

... and increased local autonomy and private sector participation.

Today, the average range, level, and quality of water services provided in most OECD countries is quite impressive. While most water and wastewater systems remain publicly owned, there is a growing industry of private service providers that compete for the right to finance, build, manage, and operate facilities. Another trend is towards management autonomy by water utilities, reflecting a shift in the role of governments away from being the "provider" of water services and towards being the "regulator". While this trend has generally been accompanied by an increased role for the private sector, ownership responsibility most often remains in public hands. The most widely used system has been the "concession" model, under which private companies with access to finances and technical know-how operate and manage publicly owned water utilities.

Harnessing science and technology is also important...

Many new scientific and technological developments have been helping to increase the efficiency of use of available water resources, to reduce emissions of pollutants to water bodies, and to improve purification of drinking water. The OECD has worked extensively on the development of technological advances in this last area. Inadequate drinking water supply and poor water quality and sanitation are among the main causes of preventable morbidity and mortality in the world.

... particularly for improved drinking water quality.

Some 5 million deaths a year are due to polluted drinking water, with infants and children particularly at risk. While the majority of these deaths occur in developing countries, OECD countries are not immune to outbreaks of water-borne disease. Major outbreaks of gastrointestinal illness have occurred in the last decade in some OECD countries. The development and use of reliable drinking water management systems and technologies are essential in assuring the microbiological safety of drinking water supplies.

OECD countries also contribute to resolving water problems that are more global in nature.

Meeting the huge financing needs for the maintenance and expansion of basic water services is a key priority recognised in the Millennium Development Goals and at the World Summit on Sustainable Development. An estimated USD 75 billion per year is needed to expand water service infrastructure, beyond the costs of maintaining existing systems. Total development assistance allocations to the water sector have been averaging about USD 3 billion a year, with an additional USD 1-1.5 billion in the form of non-concessional lending. Clearly, there is a large financing gap.

The OECD continues to work towards better water management and the achievement of internationally agreed water goals.

The OECD is undertaking a number of activities to enhance water management policies in OECD and non-OECD countries alike, basing this work on recent experiences. Much of this work supports internationally agreed water goals, including those on access to drinking water and sanitation. Current projects involve:

- Comparing performances of OECD country water management systems, using the results of OECD Environmental Performance Reviews, as well as peer reviews of country regulatory reforms and economic development.
- Addressing social issues related to water pricing policies, including the need to alleviate negative distributive effects.
- Assessing the utility of transferable permits in managing water use and pollution.
- Strengthening management and technical systems to assure microbiological drinking water quality.

- Measuring and managing water use and water pollution in agriculture.
- Supporting the development of stable financing plans for water and wastewater infrastructure expansion and maintenance in selected non-OECD countries.
- Assessing levels and effectiveness of aid for the water sector in selected non-OECD countries.

PART I

Key Challenges in Water Management

Introduction

Although OECD countries have made considerable progress in recent years in improving many aspects of their water management activities, significant challenges remain. The greatest progress has been in cleaning up the worst polluted surface water bodies, reducing industrial pollution to waterways, decoupling rates of water use from those of economic and population growth, and providing regulatory and water charging structures that promote the protection and wise use of water resources. The remaining challenges for OECD countries involve, most notably, reducing non-point sources of water pollution (*e.g.* agricultural run-off) and reversing groundwater pollution.

Outside of OECD countries, the problems are even greater. Almost 50 countries worldwide – accounting for one-third of the world's population are classified as suffering from medium-high or high water stress.* An estimated one-fifth of the world's population, or 1.1 billion people, still do not have access to safe drinking water supply, and one-third (2.4 billion people) lack adequate sanitation facilities (WHO-UNICEF, 2000). About 5 million people die each year from water-related diseases. By 2025, an estimated two-thirds of the world's population may be living in countries that face water shortages.

Water resources face competing demands from uses to support human health, economic development, and environmental services. The United Nations Committee on Economic, Social, and Cultural Rights has declared access to water a human right, emphasising that water is a social and cultural good, as well as an economic commodity (27 November 2002, Geneva). In addition, many ecosystems depend on minimum water flows to continue functioning. In this sense, water is the perfect example of a sustainable development challenge – encompassing environmental, economic, and social dimensions. Reconciling these three aspects through appropriate water management is a significant policy challenge for governments. While water management practices need to be tailored to suit local circumstances – be they

---

* Water stress is considered medium-high (or high) when the ratio of water withdrawals minus water returns to the stock of renewable water resources exceeds 20% (or 40%).

the competing demands for water, local charging structures, or income disparities – several common international objectives and principles have been agreed.

In particular, in Goal 7 of the Millennium Development Goals, over 150 countries agreed in 2000 to "halve, by 2015, the proportion of people without sustainable access to safe drinking water". Building on this, one of the targets agreed in the Plan of Implementation of the World Summit on Sustainable Development in Johannesburg in 2002 was to "halve, by the year 2015, the proportion of people who do not have access to basic sanitation". These two goals imply assuring access to safe drinking water to a further half billion people worldwide, and access to basic sanitation to a further 1.2 billion people. The estimated investments needed to meet the goal on access to water amount to USD 14-30 billion a year, in addition to the roughly USD 30 billion already being spent (UN WEHAB Working Group, 2002). While the benefits of these investments – in terms of reductions in waterborne diseases, better health, and reduced mortality – are likely to far exceed their costs, significant efforts will be needed worldwide to mobilise the funds. Some of the experiences of OECD countries in managing water resources sustainably and efficiently, while still assuring continued water security and adequate access to water services, may be of use in supporting these efforts.

This section elaborates on challenges in the water sector, emphasising the role of water in contributing to environmental, economic, and social goals as seen from the OECD perspective. Chapter 1 highlights some recent trends in water use and pollution, and the key issues involved, drawing largely from analysis in the *OECD Environmental Outlook* (OECD 2001a). Chapter 2 reviews some of the experiences and general trends in water management in OECD countries, summarising the results of *Water Management: Performance and Challenges in OECD Countries* (OECD, 2003a), a study that draws together lessons from the OECD Environmental Performance Reviews' chapters on water.

ISBN 92-64-09948 4
Improving Water Management
Recent OECD Experience
© OECD 2003

Chapter 1

Key Trends and Challenges

Context

Water is a unique raw material, essential for both life itself and for water-based economic activity. Water is also a complex and fragile resource that must be economised, managed, and protected. Freshwater resources are quite different from other natural resources, such as ore and oil deposits, in that they can be both renewable and non-renewable. While sufficient levels of precipitation and natural recharge of aquifers make surface water and groundwater renewable resources, once this natural cycle is disturbed by climatic changes, over-abstraction, or water pollution from human activities, they can become non-renewable (or "renewable" over only very long periods). Water of sufficient quality and quantity, delivered at the appropriate time, is vital for maintaining ecosystems such as wetlands, rivers, lakes, estuaries, and groundwater-dependent ecosystems. The arrangements under which water resources are allocated and managed, in terms of both quantity and quality, are therefore significant determinants of whether such ecosystems function properly.

It is therefore important to distinguish at the outset two main dimensions of water management: i) water as a *natural resource* that is an integral part of the natural ecosystem; and ii) water as the key element of *water services,* which are generally infrastructure-intensive. The first dimension involves the abstraction of water and its allocation among competing uses (*e.g.* industry, agriculture, municipal water supply, and ecological, aesthetic and recreational purposes). It also involves protection of surface-water bodies and groundwater reservoirs from degradation. The second dimension involves investment, operation and management of the infrastructure systems, and delivery of water services to final customers (*i.e.* treatment and distribution of piped water, wastewater collection and treatment, and irrigation networks).

Throughout the 20th century, population growth, combined with increased urbanisation, expanding human activities, and the need to assure the environmental integrity of ecosystems, contributed to an explosion in demand for water services. This trend is expected to continue into the foreseeable future. Population growth will probably add 2.5 to 3 billion people to the earth over the next 25 years. In 1950, 30% of the world's population lived in urban areas. In 1995, the share was nearly 45%. Today, more people live in cities than in rural areas. By 2015, one in five people will live in big cities, compared to one in nine today (Catley-Carlson, 1999).

In developing countries, urban populations will have doubled by 2025. This will put considerable stress on already-strained water supply systems. Many towns and cities in developing countries have unreliable piped water systems and experience regular supply interruptions. Furthermore, the quality of services provided by existing systems is deteriorating, chiefly because of fast rates of population growth and urbanisation, high capital costs of infrastructure, and diminishing government resources for addressing urban water issues. Existing systems also often suffer from inefficient design and operation. Thus it is imperative to learn from available experiences, especially given the high costs of water-related infrastructure.

Freshwater abstraction and water scarcity

Global water withdrawal has increased significantly over the last few decades, in part because of increasing population pressures but also because of significant increases in per capita water use. Over the last 50 years, global water withdrawal has quadrupled while the total world population roughly doubled. The Reference Scenario developed by the OECD for its Environmental Outlook to 2020 (OECD, 2001a) envisaged global water withdrawal increasing by 31% between 1995 and 2020.

There are significant regional differences in freshwater use. East Asia, Latin America, Africa and several other regions use about one-third as much water per person as the average for OECD countries, and almost one-fifth of what is used in North America. There are also significant variations within the OECD, with annual use in Denmark, Luxembourg, the Czech Republic, the Slovak Republic, and the UK, for instance, at 180 m^3 per capita or less, while the US consumes almost ten times this amount (Figure 1.1).

Overall, however, per capita water use has fallen in OECD regions by almost 11% since 1980, with just over half of all OECD countries achieving a net decrease (OECD, 1998a). This indicates an encouraging trend in decoupling water consumption from economic growth. Although per capita water abstraction has been declining in many countries, the effect of net growth in population levels has resulted in increasing total absolute abstraction in most OECD countries. Only nine OECD countries – primarily in Europe – reduced their total water abstraction between 1980 and 1997 (OECD, 1999a).

Under the OECD Reference Scenario, per capita water withdrawal is expected to remain relatively stable for OECD countries overall between 1995 and 2020, with some decreases in North America (Figure 1.2). Central and Eastern Europe is the OECD region that is likely to see the largest growth in water withdrawals in the period up to 2020, due to expected increases in per capita use combined with high population growth. Regional variations in the

Figure 1.1   **Sewerage and sewage treatment connection rates in OECD countries (latest year available)**

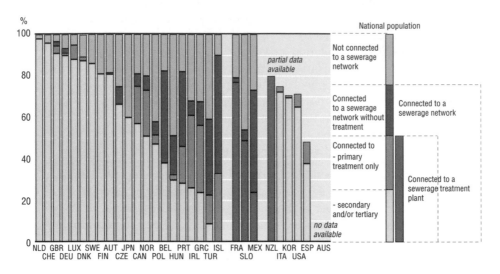

Source: OECD (2003a).

Figure 1.2   **Water withdrawals per capita (1980-2020)**

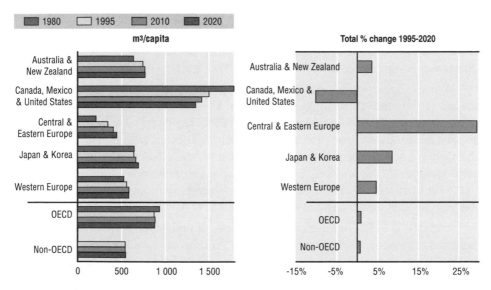

Source: OECD (1999a) and (2001a).

growth of per capita water use will to some extent balance the current disparities in use among OECD regions.

Water use per person in non-OECD regions is also expected to remain relatively stable, at levels far below the average for OECD regions. In some developing countries, per capita consumption is less than 20 litres a day, and domestic water use in some areas at less than 5 litres per person a day.

Globally, agriculture is responsible for about 69% of total freshwater abstraction (Figure 1.3). The corresponding figure for OECD countries is 45%. Worldwide agricultural demand for water is projected to increase substantially over the next few decades, as much of the additional food that will be needed to feed the world's growing population is expected to come from irrigated land. While agriculture is likely to remain the primary abstractor of freshwater in the near future, the OECD Reference Scenario to 2020 (OECD, 2001a) indicates that industry will be the fastest growing water user overall, largely due to rapid industrialisation in many non-OECD countries.

Figure 1.3   **Water withdrawals by sector (1995-2020)**

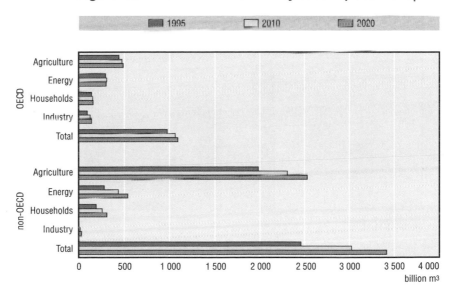

Source: OECD (2001a).

Over the past 20 years, there has been a continuous upward trend in water use for irrigation in many OECD countries, associated with an increase in irrigated land area that has been mainly encouraged by government investment in irrigation infrastructure and by irrigation water subsidies. For most countries, irrigation water represents over 80% of total agricultural water use, with much of the remainder being accounted for by livestock farming (OECD, 2001b).

Considerable improvements have been made in the efficiency of irrigation systems of many OECD countries in recent years (Figure 1.4). These gains have generally been realised either in water conveyance systems (*e.g.* reduced leakage) or through advanced and better calibrated application systems (*e.g.* drip irrigation). It is expected that irrigation water use may stabilise or even decline in many OECD countries over the next two decades. However, future trends in agricultural use will partly depend on reforms to agricultural water charges, including the extent to which these charges cover construction and maintenance costs for irrigation infrastructure.

Figure 1.4   **Share of total irrigated crop area using different irrigation systems (mid-/late 1990s)**

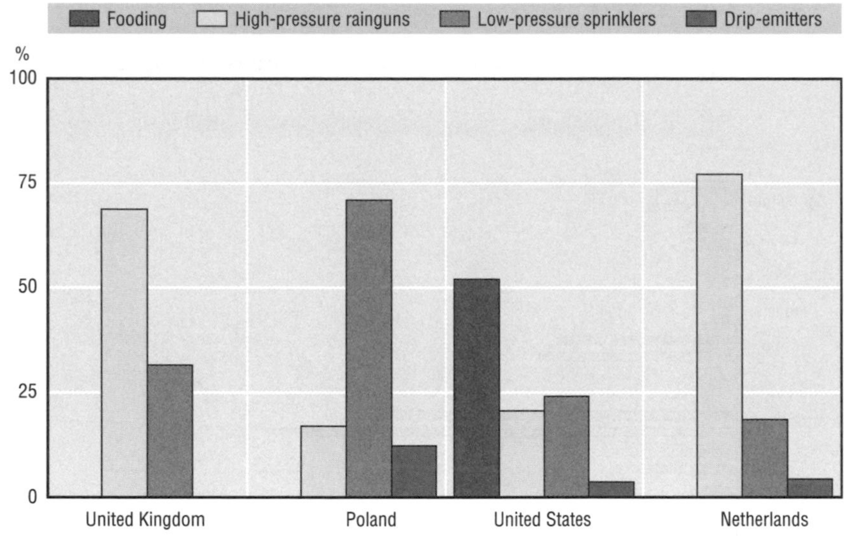

Source: OECD (2001b).

Industry accounts for 23% of global water abstraction, weighted towards the OECD countries but with industrial use in developing countries growing. Industry is the fastest growing user of freshwater resources worldwide, and demand from this sector is expected to more than double over the next two decades. The remaining 8% of global water abstraction is used by households.

Industrial abstraction has declined in OECD countries in recent years. This trend is primarily the result of increased water use efficiency but may also reflect a shift of some water-intensive industry to non-OECD countries. The most water-intensive industries include pulp and paper, chemicals, and food and beverages. Another important emerging trend in many OECD countries is the growing use of freshwater for cooling in electricity production (OECD, 1999a). The OECD Reference Scenario sees water withdrawal for energy use almost doubling worldwide over 1995-2020.

Water scarcity can have direct negative effects on human health, the economy, and the environment. The global per capita availability of freshwater has fallen dramatically, from 17 000 m^3 a year in 1950, to 7 300 m^3 in 1995. This change has been largely due to increased population, but it has also been influenced by the decline in availability of uncontaminated freshwater resources. Current trends indicate that the level of per capita available water resources is likely to decline even further. An estimated 47 countries, representing approximately one-third of the world's population, are already classified as suffering medium-high or high water stress. The proportion is expected to double by 2025.

Because freshwater resources are distributed very unevenly within and among countries, and the pressures on these resources are also unevenly distributed, water scarcity can significantly affect one region, even while a neighbouring region has abundant freshwater. Even within OECD countries, development is restricted by water scarcity in extensive arid or semi-arid areas. A perverse effect of the under-pricing of water services to households and industry is that is can encourage development in water-scarce areas unable to support the accompanying demands for water.

As areas of scarcity in surface water resources emerge, countries are increasingly drawing on their groundwater aquifers. In most OECD countries, irrigation using surface water has reached its maximum feasible limit, and abstraction is more and more from groundwater sources. However, most aquifers are replenished slowly: the average recharge rate ranges from 0.1% to 0.3% a year. As a result, groundwater abstraction is beginning to exceed replenishment in some locations. Worldwide, 17 countries are "mining" their groundwater reserves – that is, extracting more water annually than is naturally recharged) (WRI *et al.*, 1999). Over-abstraction of groundwater can have significant environmental effects, including land subsidence, lowering of water tables, and intrusion of seawater, which contaminates the freshwater resources with salt and causes salinisation of coastal agricultural lands (UNEP, 2000).

Freshwater quality and water pollution

Pollution of water bodies further limits the water available for human use. It also degrades ecosystems and impairs their ability to provide valuable services. The discharge of inadequately treated sewage in large cities causes deoxygenation and can lead to ammonia toxicity, while nitrate pollution can stimulate rapid algal growth in waterways, leading to eutrophication in both inland waters and the sea (UNEP, 1997; UNEP, 2000). Many algae produce toxins that, once ingested by molluscs and fish, either kill or accumulate in them, endangering their predators in turn (WRI *et al.*, 1994). Industrial waste can lead to contamination with heavy metals (*e.g.* lead, mercury, and cadmium) and persistent organic compounds. Airborne pollution can also be detrimental to water quality. For example, hundreds of lakes in Scandinavia suffer from acidification, largely due to past sulphur and nitrogen emissions from fossil fuel combustion. The situation is even more serious in developing countries, where trends point to accelerating contamination of available water supplies, especially in rapidly urbanising areas.

Despite major efforts to clean up many of the worst polluted water bodies over the last few decades, few OECD countries meet the baseline quality standard (*e.g.* suitability for fishing and swimming) for all inland waters. Most OECD countries are also having particular difficulties protecting groundwater quality, especially from non-point-source pollution such as agricultural run-off or arsenic from mining. Nitrate concentrations (most commonly linked to livestock waste and fertiliser use) exceeding World Health Organization (WHO) drinking water guidelines are now widespread in European and some North American aquifers. Available evidence suggests a trend towards worsening aquifer water quality in several parts of the OECD. Once groundwater is contaminated, it can be very difficult to clean up; the rate of flow is usually very slow, and purification measures are often costly. Existing regulations and policies to address surface water pollution are likely to prove effective, but the lack of comprehensive plans to manage groundwater resources and address non-point-source pollution will probably result in continuing contamination of aquifers over the next few decades.

Agriculture is a major contributor to OECD water quality problems (Box 1.1). The principal sources of water pollution from agriculture are nutrients (mainly livestock waste and inorganic fertiliser), pesticides, and soil sediments. Acidification, salinisation, biological contamination and heavy metals associated with agriculture are also problematic in some countries and sub-national regions. In several OECD countries, agriculture accounts for more than 40% of all nitrogenous emissions and over 30% of phosphorous emissions into surface water (OECD, 2001b). Although agriculture-related nutrient surpluses from fertiliser use and livestock waste are declining in most OECD countries, the contribution of agriculture to total water contamination is still growing.

In most OECD countries, considerable effort has been made to reduce emissions of pollutants from agriculture into surface waters, aquifers, and the

---

Box 1.1. **Water quality indicators in agriculture**

OECD countries are developing two approaches to measuring the impact of agriculture on water quality: "risk" and "state" indicators, with the emphasis on nitrates and phosphorus. Risk indicators estimate the potential contamination of water originating from agricultural activities. State indicators measure the actual trends in concentrations of pollutants in water, against a threshold level, in areas vulnerable to pollution from agriculture. Risk indicators are used in a number of countries, partly because monitoring the state of water quality can be costly and difficult, especially in terms of distinguishing between the contribution of agriculture and that of other sources (such as industry).

Risk indicators, developed by drawing on a range of existing data, such as nutrient balances, help provide an indirect measure of the impact of nitrate and phosphorus losses from agriculture to water. The indicators have been useful in revealing overall national trends in risk on nutrient contamination as well as differences at regional level.

Source: OECD (2001b).

sea (Figure 1.5). Nevertheless, the level of these pollutants is still too high, especially in regions with intensive farming. Agriculture is not the only sector that burdens aquatic environments with pollutants, but for many countries it is still a major contributor.

The extent of groundwater pollution from agricultural nutrients is less well documented than for surface and marine waters, largely because the sampling costs are higher. Moreover, correlating nutrient contamination levels in groundwater with changes in farming practices and production systems is difficult because it can take many years for nutrients to leach into aquifers. As for pesticides, while their use has decreased in many OECD countries since the mid-1980s, the long time lag between their use and detection in groundwater means that (as with nitrates) the situation could deteriorate before it starts to improve.

Projections indicate that while agriculture will remain by far the dominant source of biochemical oxygen demand (BOD) and nitrogen loading to waterways for some time, both in OECD regions and worldwide, emissions from the sector in OECD regions will increase at a slower rate to 2020 than in the past (Figure 1.6). Recent trends in soil erosion losses in OECD countries indicate that soil sediment deposition in waterways continues to be a serious problem in many countries, though it is generally declining.

Figure 1.5   **Share of agriculture in total emissions of nitrogen and phosphorus into surface waters (mid-1990s)**

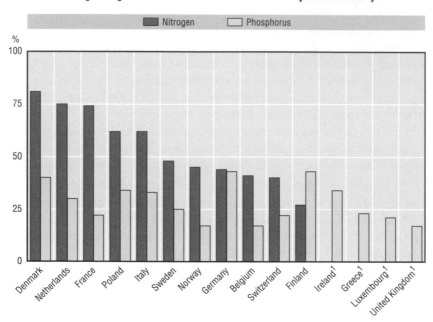

1. Data for nitrogen emissions are not available.
Source: OECD (2001b).

Industry is a relatively small contributor to BOD loading to waterways, but for other pollutants it remains one of the largest sources of emissions to water resources in OECD countries, and industrial pollution of watercourses worldwide could quadruple by 2025 (SEI, 1997). The effects of industrial pollution on the aquatic environment vary considerably, depending on the types and quantities of substances released. Industrial sites can be particularly important point sources of pollution to watercourses because of their size, even if the substances they emit are innocuous in smaller quantities. Some industrial processes (*e.g.* power generation) can also result in environmental degradation by heating water, which reduces dissolved oxygen while accelerating oxygen-demanding biochemical processes. In response to increasing regulation of industrial emissions, industries in OECD countries have had to develop better and safer wastewater disposal systems, often using in-house purification before releasing wastewater back to the environment (if it is of sufficient quality) or to a wastewater treatment plant. The use of technologies to reduce air emissions has also helped reduce industrial water pollution; for instance, using sulphur scrubbers in coal-burning plants decreases the acidification of surface water bodies.

Figure 1.6 **Emissions of water pollutants by sector (1995-2020)**

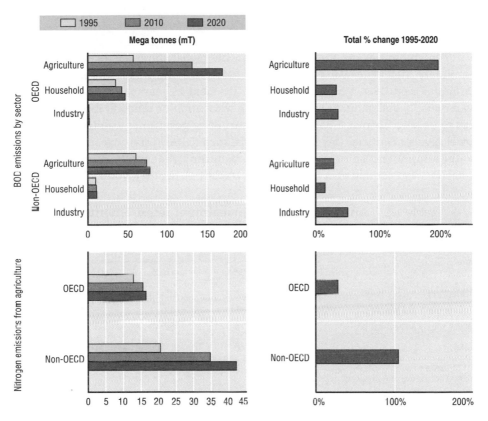

Source: OECD (2001a).

Pollution from industry and urban centres is a significant indirect cause of degradation of water bodies and land. In addition to degrading the ecological value of water bodies, it increases the risk of exposure to toxic chemicals and pathogens, either directly or through consumption of contaminated fish and shellfish. While developed countries have largely been able to manage industrial and municipal wastewater discharges effectively, most wastewater in developing countries still goes untreated into local watercourses.

The main factors in municipal water pollution abatement in OECD countries are increases in the number of households connected to basic sewage treatment facilities and the use of biological or other advanced treatment technologies. With continuing expansion of secondary and tertiary wastewater treatment systems, OECD household contributions to BOD in freshwater systems are expected to increase by only 15% to 2020. However,

BOD loading from households in non-OECD countries is expected to rise by over twice that (OECD, 2001a).

Financing

The amount of investment needed in the global water sector remains extremely high. The *World Water Vision* (Cosgrove and Rijsberman, 2000) estimated that USD 75 billion a year over the next 25 years was needed for water supply and sanitation, not counting renovation or rehabilitation. This has to be seen against a background of shrinking government budgets and lower levels of Official Development Assistance (ODA). Total investment in water supply and sanitation in 1995 – excluding that made directly by industry – was estimated at USD 30 billion (Table 1.1). In other words, the level

Table 1.1. **Annual worldwide investment requirements for water resources**

Area	Billions of USD		Share (%)	
	1995	2025[1]	1995	2025[1]
Agriculture	30–35	30	43-50	17
Environment and industry	10–15	75	13-21	41
Water supply and sanitation	30	75	38-43	42
Total	70–80	180	100	100

1. Estimates.
Source: Cosgrove and Rijsberman (2000).

of investment needs to more than double. The situation is most serious in the developing countries, especially those undergoing rapid urbanisation, but considerable investment will be required in many OECD countries as well.

As for the financing of the Millennium Development Goal of halving the population without access to safe drinking water by 2015, it is unclear how much this will cost. The Water Supply and Sanitation Collaborative Council and the Global Water Partnership have estimated that between USD 14 billion and USD 30 billion a year would be required, in addition to the approximately USD 30 billion already being spent, to achieve the target on access to safe drinking water (UN WEHAB Working Group, 2002).

Many water supply and treatment facilities receive insufficient funds for management, operation, and maintenance. This means they seldom operate at full efficiency, which accelerates their deterioration and thus increases rehabilitation costs. In recent years, major efforts in many OECD countries have reduced water leakage rates in municipal water service networks.

Leakage is now as low as 10-12% in some countries, although it remains high in others (OECD, 1998b). Significant investments will nonetheless be required to maintain the improved rates and to reduce leakage in countries where problems remain.

Equity

Many of the social issues involved in water management can be considered in terms of "equity". The most obvious of these is equity among *income groups*. It is generally accepted that charges for at least basic water services (including sewerage) should be affordable to all. The implication is that poorer consumers should not have to pay a disproportionately larger part of their disposable income for water services than better-off consumers do.

Equity issues can also be considered in terms of *consumer types* (*i.e.* higher- or lower-volume consumption levels). It is important to distinguish this aspect from equity among income groups, as low-income households are not necessarily low-consumption customers. Low-income families may be large in size or live in multi-family housing units with shared water taps. Thus, measures to provide preferential treatment to lower-consumption water customers could unintentionally penalise low-income (but larger) families.

Equity can also be considered in terms of *disparity among regions as regards access to water services*. Such disparities have two distinct causes. The first is related to the naturally uneven distribution of water resources around the world due to differing hydrologic, geologic, climatic and other natural conditions. Variations in water prices and charges reflecting differences in scarcity and in production and delivery costs are thus to be expected. The second cause of disparity in access to water supply and sanitation is simply the fact that optimal service coverage has not yet been reached. There is some evidence of continuing disparities of this type among OECD regions, particularly as concerns urban vs. rural areas or underdeveloped regions. Furthermore, the transboundary nature of water resources can lead to geographical inequity in terms of access and quality.

Finally, *intergenerational equity* should be considered. For water resource management to be sustainable, consumption levels today must not unduly reduce future generations' opportunities to benefit from water resources.

Access and affordability

Access to public water supply, especially in urban areas, is no longer a serious problem in most OECD countries, with at least three-quarters of the total population (and often more than 90%) already being served. Thus, the basic social and public health requirements for "universal access" have largely been fulfilled (OECD, 1999b). Economic considerations dictate that 100% coverage will never be attained, because it is simply inappropriate in many situations for rural consumers to be connected. A few OECD countries have yet to connect the whole population that could economically be linked to the public water supply. Those not connected rely on sources such as private wells, public water fountains, and private water vendors. In other OECD countries, the need to upgrade ageing networks appears to be emerging at the same time as new demands for higher standards of drinking water purification (OECD, 1998c).

The total share of the population connected to public wastewater treatment plants in OECD countries rose from 51% in 1980 to an average of 65% in the late 1990s, although connection rates vary from a low of under 10% to a high of almost 100% (Figure 1.1). In many countries, the "economic limit" has been reached, and alternatives need to be found for sanitation in small, isolated communities whose connection to the main sewerage system is not economically feasible. Households not connected to public systems increasingly have private individual sewage treatment.

OECD studies (OECD, 2003b) suggest that water and sanitation prices have increased in some OECD countries and are likely to continue to do so. As a result, about half of OECD countries show evidence that affordability of water charges for low-income households is a significant issue now, or might become one if appropriate measures are not taken.

The global situation is more worrying. According to the WHO, 1.1 billion people do not have access to safe drinking water supply and 2.4 billion people lack adequate sanitation facilities (WHO-UNICEF, 2000). In other words, at least one-fifth of the world population does not have access to safe drinking water, and almost one-third lacks adequate sanitation. For all low-income countries, it is estimated that just 45% of the population is connected to improved sanitation facilities (World Bank, 2002). About 90% of all wastewater in the developing world goes untreated into local watercourses. The low sanitation coverage is attributed to a combination of factors, including the comparatively high cost of sanitation systems and the commercial risks associated with managing this type of service.

Even these figures give an optimistic picture, since they imply that the services that are available are used effectively. If the real effectiveness of all water supply and sanitation systems were mapped, it would likely be clear that many people who appear to have access to the systems do not in reality. While significant progress has been made to provide access to adequate drinking water services, access to adequate sanitation services is much more limited, and remains an urgent challenge in much of the world.

Slum-dwellers often have to buy water from vendors at several times the price of piped water. They also face additional costs, which may not always be explicitly financial (*e.g.* time or distance). Because of disease risks, they must often boil their water, which translates into higher fuel costs and increased air pollution. In some countries, demand for fuel wood to boil water contributes significantly to forest depletion and watershed degradation. Furthermore, boiling does not eliminate contamination from heavy metals, other inorganic pollutants, and many industrial organic pollutants.

Many poor households would be able and willing to pay the full costs of water supply infrastructure and services (in cash or in kind) at the community level, and possibly at the household level. However, difficulties in obtaining recognition of housing or land tenure rights can seriously limit access by the urban poor to adequate water and sanitation services (OECD, 2002h)

Other social challenges

Some 2 million children worldwide die every year from *water-related diseases* and many more suffer health problems and disabilities related to poor water quality. In the poorest countries, one in five children dies before the age of 5, mainly from infectious diseases related to insufficiency of water quantity and quality (UN WEHAB Working Group, 2002). Many water-related health threats exist only in developing countries and result from problems that are virtually unknown today in industrialised countries.

If the provision of safe drinking water and sanitation services to more than 1 billion people is among the most critical challenges for sustainable development, accompanying improvements in hygiene will also be essential. Improved hygiene is a critical factor in combating diarrhoeal diseases and intestinal-worm infestations that cause sickness and death among children. Improved water and sanitation can reduce episodes of diarrhoea by up to 40%, deaths by up to 60%, and child stunting by up to 50%. The simple act of washing hands can reduce diarrhoeal episodes by up to 33%, while food hygiene can reduce them by up to 70%. Convenient access to safe water alone can reduce episodes of diarrhoea by up to 15%. When such steps are fully integrated into health and education programmes, the overall benefits can be significant (UN WEHAB Working Group, 2002).

Concern over the greater vulnerability of children, the elderly, and those with weakened immune systems to infections by viruses and parasites that are often highly resistant to chlorine disinfection is creating demand for more advanced microbiological purification. Remaining lead piping in older buildings and cities is another health concern, as is the effect of disinfectants and disinfection by-products on drinking water.

Social and cultural norms frequently result in *gender differences* in practices relating to the use of water resources. In the developing world, women traditionally play central roles as users, providers, and managers of water in the household. They are also typically responsible for hygiene. They dispose of household waste, maintain sanitation facilities, and educate children in hygiene. They also play an important (but often invisible) role in the maintenance of water quality. In rural areas, women are involved in subsistence farming and small-scale livestock production, activities that depend heavily on access to, and availability, of water.

It is therefore important to involve women fully in demand-driven water supply and sanitation programmes, including at the planning and decision-making levels, as communities decide what type of systems they want and are willing to help finance. Consciously addressing gender roles and priorities, especially by using gender analysis, can help increase project sustainability and equality of access to water resources. Looking beyond gender-specific uses of household water to take into consideration women's productive use of water in growing crops and raising animals and produce for the market requires sensitisation of women's contributions to the economy (Box 1.2).

Box 1.2. **Water and gender: selected priorities**

- The specific needs of women for water should come more clearly into focus, in particular those related to small-scale activities (gardening, small-scale livestock production, and domestic uses) that are vital for the household.

- The design and location of water supply and sanitation facilities should better reflect the needs of both women and men.

- Adopted technologies should better reflect women's needs (*e.g.* hand pumps should be easy for women and children to use).

- Technical and financial planning for operation and maintenance of water supply and sanitation facilities should be improved, and women should play a role in this activity.

Source: Adapted from OECD (2002b).

ISBN 92-64-09948-4
Improving Water Management
Recent OECD Experience
© OECD 2003

Chapter 2

Meeting the Challenges: Recent OECD Experience

OECD context

In all OECD countries, the water sector (*i.e.* activities related to the withdrawal, purification, and distribution of water for household, industrial, and agricultural use, as well as to the treatment and disposal of effluents and the protection of water resources) represents a major part of the economy. Geographic, climatic, economic, and other factors are responsible for the wide variation among countries regarding the size of the sector and the relative importance of subsectors such as supply, purification, treatment, irrigation, and drainage. For OECD countries as a whole, about 40% of total pollution abatement and control (PAC) investments and operating expenditure relate to water (*i.e.* sewerage and wastewater treatment). Water-related PAC expenditure ranges from 0.3% to 1% of country GDP, including both public and private expenditure (*i.e.* that part of industry and households that treat their own wastewater) (OECD, 2003a).

In the *OECD Environmental Strategy for the First Decade of the 21st Century*, Environment Ministers called for action at both the national and international levels to address the challenges of assuring adequate availability of freshwater for all uses (human health, economic development, ecosystems) and the protection of water bodies (Box 2.1). Successful implementation of this strategy will ultimately depend on co-operation with non-OECD countries, including developing countries and countries with economies in transition. OECD countries have an important role to play by helping other countries build capacity and by working with them to develop effective and equitable arrangements for addressing global environmental problems, recognising the common but differentiated responsibilities between richer and poorer countries. Active partnerships will also need to be sought with the private sector and civil society.

The OECD has also identified a framework of the key elements necessary for achieving sustainable development (OECD, 2001c):

- *Make wider use of markets*. There is significant scope for expanded use of market-based approaches to provide signals to internalise environmental and social externalities efficiently. On the environment side, this is likely to involve more use of environmental taxes, tradable permits, and subsidy reforms.

Box 2.1. **OECD Environmental Strategy: freshwater (extract)**

Challenges:

- Manage the use of freshwater resources and associated watersheds so as to maintain adequate supply of freshwater of suitable quality for human use and to support aquatic and other ecosystems.

- Protect, restore and prevent deterioration of all bodies of surface water and groundwater to ensure the achievement of water quality objectives in OECD countries.

National action by OECD countries:

1. Ensure access for all to safe drinking water and adequate sanitation.

2. Achieve agreed water quality targets and adopt additional targets necessary to ensure the ecological value of in-situ water resources and the ecological functions they provide.

3. Apply the ecosystem approach to the management of freshwater resources and associated watersheds, based on integrated river basin management.

4. Develop and apply legal frameworks supported by appropriate policy instruments to ensure the sustainable use of freshwater resources, including measures to enhance their efficient use.

5. Establish policies aimed at recovering the full costs of water services provision and the external costs associated with water use, and provide incentives to use water resources efficiently (demand side management), taking the social impacts of such policies into account.

6. Significantly reduce water network leakage.

7. Develop appropriate strategies to manage watersheds ecologically to prevent extreme flood and drought risk.

8. Ensure co-operation for the environmentally sound management and efficient use of transboundary water resources to reduce flood risks and to minimise potential conflicts from the use or pollution of transboundary water resources.

9. Provide support for capacity building and technology transfer to assist developing countries in managing and developing their freshwater resources in a sustainable manner, and in ensuring safe drinking water and adequate sanitation.

Source: OECD (2001d).

- *Strengthen decision-making processes.* Better policy co-ordination at all levels of government could improve the efficiency and effectiveness of government actions. Among other things, this implies better integration of environmental and social policy needs into sectoral economic policies, improved transparency and democratic participation in policy design and implementation, and stronger efforts to co-ordinate policy at the international level.

- *Harness science and technology.* Scientific progress and technological development are major forces underlying rising productivity and living standards. This fact suggests that a business environment is needed in which suitable incentives exist for technological innovation and diffusion. Over the long term, the implication is that government would take a strong role in basic research activities, leaving applied research largely to the private sector.

- *Manage links to the global economy.* The global economy involves two policy areas of particular concern for sustainable development: i) international trade and investment flows; and ii) the needs of developing countries as participants in global economic activity. One major implication of these issues for sustainable development policy is that trade and investment flows need to be as compatible as possible with environmental and social policy objectives. Another is that achieving global sustainable development will not be possible without the active participation of developing countries.

This framework, when applied to natural resource (including water) management, yields the following broad priorities for policy action:

- ❖ Facilitating the development of property rights and markets.
- ❖ Removing subsidies that hamper sustainable resource use.
- ❖ Reducing resource degradation and enhancing the provision of environmental services.
- ❖ Improving the management of publicly owned natural resources.
- ❖ Reducing pollution by resource-based industries.
- ❖ Addressing distributive implications of natural resource management policies.

A major challenge facing many OECD countries in their management of water resources is agricultural water use and associated pollution. Irrigation water is free or heavily subsidised in most OECD countries. Run-off from agricultural activities is a significant contributor to surface- and groundwater quality problems due to nitrate and phosphorus pollution, contamination with pesticides, and the harmful effects of soil sediment and mineral salts. Many OECD countries are developing policies specifically aimed at managing agricultural water use and pollution in the context of the sustainable development framework (Box 2.2).

Box 2.2. **Applying the sustainable development framework to water issues: experiences with agricultural reforms**

Agricultural policy reform: When carefully targeted, the reform of agricultural policies can help reduce distortions in agricultural production and the use of water resources, improve water quality, and enhance environmental benefits associated with water use in agriculture.

Transparency: Improved transparency of water management policies can help identify the full economic, environmental, and social costs and benefits of water use in agriculture, and any associated transfers between farmers, taxpayers, and consumers. All relevant stakeholders, including local communities and farmers, should be involved in water policy design and management.

Cost-benefit analysis: Alternatives to major new or replacement investments in water projects should be considered; and where such projects are deemed necessary, cost-benefit analyses that consider economic, environmental, hydrological, and social factors should be carried out.

Indicators and information: Improved information on agri-environmental processes resulting from links between agriculture, water, and environment can support decision-making. Increased funding of public and private research and development, and the dissemination of information to farmers, is needed.

Water rights: Water rights systems need to be clarified in many countries and mechanisms set up to facilitate trade in water rights in order to strengthen the legal framework and institutions that enable the efficient allocation and use of water.

Institutions and policy coherence: Innovative approaches and appropriate institutional frameworks are needed to integrate agricultural, regional, and water policies.

Water pricing: Mechanisms can be used to introduce or strengthen pricing, charging, and allocation methods for agricultural users and beneficiaries of water. These mechanisms need to reflect the economic and environmental costs and benefits, and take into account local social conditions. Where support to farmers is deemed necessary, it should be in the form of income support not linked to commodity production or past crop yield, and should be provided only as long as is necessary to meet clearly stated objectives.

Involvement of stakeholders: All stakeholders need to be involved in the design of policies and the planning and management of water resources. Thus, ways should be sought to encourage farmers, water service providers, and users to form associations aimed at improved water management and incorporating a multidisciplinary, integrated approach to water policy.

Source: OECD (1998d).

Recent developments in OECD countries

The OECD has carried out country environmental performance reviews since 1992. To date this programme has involved 42 reviews, covering all member countries and a few non-OECD countries. These reviews suggest that considerable progress has been achieved in the following broad areas (OECD, 2003a):

● Extending access to drinking water for all.

● Improving water supply and sanitation for low-income groups.

● Making major reductions in point discharges from industry and urban areas.

● Cleaning up the worst polluted waters.

● Establishing a comprehensive framework of water management laws, policies, programmes, and institutions.

● Achieving a good degree of integration of quantity and quality management.

● Making progress towards the whole-basin approach.

● Widening the implementation of integrated permitting.

● Improving enforcement of regulations and permit conditions.

● Attaining good capacity for effective implementation of policies and measures.

● Increasing momentum in the reform of water pricing regimes.

Nevertheless, water management efforts of recent decades have not been enough to safeguard and restore all receiving waters and aquatic ecosystems to adequate quality levels. Much progress remains to be made in many areas, including:

● Achievement of ambient water quality objectives.

● Better protection of aquatic ecosystems.

● Improved cost-effectiveness of water management policies and activities.

● Reduction of subsidies that exacerbate problems such as over-abstraction and pollution.

● More consistent application of the polluter pays and user pays principles.

● Implementation of existing laws, regulations, and policies.

● Renewed attention to human health aspects of water management.

● Control of diffuse sources and depositions of nutrients, heavy metals, and persistent organic pollutants.

● Prevention of aquifer contamination by nitrates, pesticides, and other persistent chemicals.

- Completion, restoration, and upgrading of wastewater treatment infrastructure.
- Better integration of water management into sectoral and land use policies.
- Protection against floods and droughts.
- Greater public participation in the formulation of water management policies and programmes.
- More effective measures to ensure that water is affordable to all.

The following sections provide some additional details on three of the "success areas" for OECD countries: reduction of point source water pollution, increased water use efficiency, and more integrated water management practices.

Reduction of point source water pollution

Many OECD countries have cleaned up the most conspicuous water pollution that initially caused public concern in the 1970s. Major organisational and financial efforts over several decades were needed to construct infrastructure capable of treating the many thousands of municipal and industrial point discharges. Industrial discharges of heavy metals and persistent chemicals have been reduced as a result by 70-90% (or more) in most cases.

Most countries have used a combination of technology-based, nationally uniform, effluent limits and receiving water standards to reduce end-of-pipe discharges. Often, the emphasis has been on the former, especially for toxic chemicals. However, because effluent is being treated to progressively higher levels, the marginal clean-up costs per pollution unit have risen, so nationally uniform effluent limits have become increasingly inefficient (because the assimilative capacity of receiving waters is not identical in all locations).

Despite these significant efforts to reduce end-of-pipe discharges, few OECD countries can yet claim to meet the baseline quality standard for all inland waters. While dissolved oxygen content in larger rivers is satisfactory during most of the year and bacterial contamination has been significantly reduced, for several water quality parameters it is not possible to discern general trends of improvement. For example, nitrate concentrations appear to have stabilised in some watersheds, probably as a result of nitrogen removal from sewerage effluents or better management of livestock waste and fertilisers, but in many rivers this positive trend cannot yet be detected.

Increased water use efficiency

Industry in OECD countries has significantly increased its efficiency of water use, reducing total industry- and energy-related use by 12% in the past two decades and increasing water recycling and reuse. To a large extent, these developments have been in response to higher industrial water charges in most OECD countries and stricter ambient water quality standards (OECD, 1999b). Some OECD countries have experienced declines in average water use at the household level, most likely reflecting the wider adoption of volume-based water charges that provide incentives for households to minimise use.

In the OECD as a whole, agriculture is responsible for about 45% of total water abstraction and in some countries the use of irrigation is still growing. Increasing competition for scarce water resources reinforces the need to allocate water to highest-value uses. This need is greatest in arid and semi-arid regions, but even where competition for off-stream uses is lower, growing demand for various in-stream uses (*e.g.* recreation and to preserve wetlands and other ecosystems) will encourage greater efficiency of water use. This trend will particularly affect agriculture, as it is the main water-using sector in many countries. Thus, the solution to many water management problems, in terms of quantity as well as quality, is strongly linked to the use of water in agriculture.

More integrated water management practices

By the 1980s, many OECD countries had thoroughly reviewed existing water laws and policies, but implementation of the associated regulations and permit conditions was not always as rigorous as it might have been. In the early 1990s, some countries revised their enforcement system to correct this shortcoming. Improvements include enforcement strategies that tie the frequency of inspections to permit holders' previous performance, and better communication procedures.

There has also been a trend away from a uniform, national approach to water management, and towards "place-based" approaches that put more emphasis on the biological quality of receiving waters and on the objectives set for their use at particular locations. Some OECD countries have had good experience with "river contracts", in which central and local governments, the private sector, and NGOs commit themselves to a set of co-ordinated actions to clean up part or all of a particular river by a certain date.

Some countries have long had river basin agencies, several are now creating them, and others are actively considering doing so. Still others, while not making the integrative river basin approach a fundamental feature of their institutional structure, are improving integration by creating *ad hoc* entities for the protection of specific water bodies, with representation by all stakeholders.

PART II

Making Markets Work
for Water Management

Introduction

OECD experience suggests that the wider use of market-based approaches can contribute significantly to the resolution of many water management problems. These approaches include policy instruments such as water use or pollution charges, tradable permits for water withdrawals or release of specific pollutants, and fines for exceeding limits. Such instruments use the price system to encourage individual water users or polluters to take into account the full environmental and social impacts of their decisions. In other words they provide economic incentives that encourage water resource users to increase their water use efficiency and to reduce unsustainable effluent levels.

In addition to studying economic instruments for environmental management in general, the OECD is carrying out work dealing specifically with the use of economic instruments in water management. *The Price of Water: Trends in OECD Countries* (OECD, 1999b) reviewed practices in OECD countries with regard to water service pricing structures and tariff levels in the household, industrial, and agricultural sectors. More recent work focuses on experiences and best practices in relation to water-related social issues such as the affordability of water services for vulnerable groups (*e.g.* low-income households and retired people). Chapter 3 summarises the results of OECD work on water pricing, including a new report on *Social Issues in the Provision and Pricing of Water Services* (OECD, 2003b).

Chapter 4 looks at experiences with market mechanisms in water resource management in non-OECD countries, primarily in Eastern Europe, the Caucasus, and Central Asia (EECCA), but also in China, drawing on the results of a forthcoming study on Guidelines for Consumer Protection and Public Participation in Urban Water Sector Reform in Eastern Europe, Caucasus and Central Asia (OECD, 2003a forthcoming). Many of these countries have serious financial deficits in the water sector, which result in under-funding of water and wastewater treatment infrastructure maintenance or expansion. These countries are often struggling to put in place water charges that cover the full economic costs of delivering water services, let alone the environmental and social costs. The chapter therefore presents lessons learned through OECD work with the EECCA countries on investment and financing strategies for water and wastewater services, including those reflected in Water Management and Investment in the New Independent States (OECD-IWA, 2001), as well as experiences with urban water service financing in China using a computer programme called FEASIBLE©.

ISBN 92-64-09948-4
Improving Water Management
Recent OECD Experience
© OECD 2003

Chapter 3

Water Pricing in OECD Countries

Tariff structures

Given the widely differing demands on water supply systems, and the different institutional and cultural frameworks within which pricing policies have to operate, it is not surprising that water pricing structures of OECD countries continue to vary considerably. In particular, the rates at which countries are moving towards marginal cost pricing, full cost recovery, and better targeting of support for low-income users vary widely.

Nevertheless, there does seem to be a general movement away from the pricing of water services solely to generate revenue, and towards the use of tariffs to achieve a wider range of economic, environmental, and social objectives. Awareness also seems to be growing about which elements of water price structures (connection charges, volumetric and fixed charges, etc.) can best achieve particular policy objectives.

The metering of water consumption is a prerequisite for the application of efficient water pricing policies. About two-thirds of OECD member countries already meter more than 90% of single-family houses, and others are expanding their metering systems (Table 3.1). On the other hand, the trend towards metering is not universal – it is still a very controversial policy issue in some contexts.

Interest has therefore been expressed in some countries in the idea of "selective metering" of houses. For example, this can involve compulsory selective metering where new water resources are scarce, where households are consuming significant amounts of "discretionary" water (*e.g.* for luxury use), and where the initial installation costs of meters are likely to be relatively low (*e.g.* new homes).

The situation in apartment blocks, where most of the OECD population lives, is more varied. Although the water supply entering apartment buildings is metered in nearly every country, only in a few countries is separate metering available for individual apartments. In most cases, the building owner or manager receives a volumetrically based water bill, and recovers this charge – together with that for wastewater services – from residents, using some flat rate criterion such as floor space. For both equity and efficiency reasons, some countries are gradually moving towards metering in individual apartments.

Table 3.2 summarises the situation with regard to household tariff structures in the public water supply system. Broadly, there is a trend away

Table 3.1. **Metering penetration in single-family houses and apartments connected to public water supply**

	Year	Metering penetration in:		
		Single-family houses	Individual apartments[1]	All individual households
Australia	1998	95-100%	"insignificant"[2]	n.a.
Austria	1998	100%	"very few"[3]	n.a.
Belgium	1997	90%	"many cases"	n.a.
Canada	1998	55%	"few"	n.a.
Czech Republic	1998	100%	n.a.	n.a.
Denmark	1996	64%	1% in Copenhagen	n.a.
Finland	1998	100%	"very low"	n.a.
France	1995	100%	> 50%	88%
Germany	1997	100%	10-20%	55-60%
Greece[4]	1998	100%	100%	100%
Hungary	1998	100%	n.a.	n.a.
Iceland	1997	0%	0%	0%
Ireland	1998	0%	0%	0%
Italy	1998	90-100%	"many examples"	<30%
Japan	1997	100%	94%	100%
Korea	1998	100%	100%	n.a.
Netherlands	1997	93%	n.a.	n.a.
New Zealand	1997	25%	n.a.	n.a.
Norway	1998	"low"	0% or "very low"	10-15%
Poland	1998	100%	0%	"about 10%"
Portugal	1998	100%	n.a.	n.a.
Spain[5]	1998	"nearly 100%"	"nearly 100%"	95%
Sweden	1998	100%	0%	"about half"
Switzerland	1998	100%	0%	n.a.
Turkey[6]	1998	"nearly 100%"	"nearly 100%"	> 95%
United Kingdom:				
Eng. and Wales	1998	12+%	"a few"	11%
N. Ireland	1997	0%	0%	0%
Scotland	1997	"near 0%"	"near 0%"	0.002%
United States	1997	90+%	n.a.	n.a.

n.a. = not available.
1. Applies to cold water metering; hot water provided in apartments via district heating is normally metered, but even here the practice varies widely.
2. "Insignificant" in Sydney only; the situation elsewhere is unknown.
3. More precisely, "perhaps about 20" apartment buildings in Vienna have individual meters.
4. Athens only.
5. Barcelona only.
6. Ankara only.
Source: OECD (1999b).

from fixed charges and towards volumetric charging. Even where fixed charges persist, there is evidence of a shift towards the reduction or even abolition of large minimum free allowances. In South Korea, for example, the

Table 3.2. Public water supply: household tariff structure (% of utilities [U] or population [P] with a given structure)

	Year	No. utilities in sample (and % of pop. represented)	Unit	Flat fee	CONSTANT VOLUMETRIC RATE			INCREASING-BLOCK SCHEDULE			DECREASING-BLOCK SCHEDULE			Normal number of blocks
					No fixed charge	Plus fixed charge	Plus fixed + min.	No fixed charge	Plus fixed charge	Plus fixed + min.	No fixed charge	Plus fixed charge	Plus fixed + min.	
Australia	2000-1	17 (72%)	P (U)	–	–	73% (12)	–	–	27% (5)	–	–	–	–	2
Austria	1999	71	U	1	5	65	–	–	–	–	–	–	–	–
Belgium														
Brussels	2001	2	U	–	–	1	–	–	1	–	–	–	–	2
Flanders	2001	17	U	–	–	–	–	–	17	–	–	4	–	2
Wallonia	2001	46	U	–	4	21	–	–	17	–	–	–	–	2
Canada	1999	1 214 (77%)	P	43%	↓	36%	↑	↓	9%	↑	↓	12%	↑	2
Denmark	2000		U, P	rural	↓	most	↑	–	–	–	–	–	–	–
Finland	2000		U, P	–	–	100%	–	–	–	–	–	–	–	–
France	1990	500	U	2%	5%	46%	47%	–	–	–	–	–	–	–
Germany	2001	1 030	U, P	–	< 5%	> 95%	–	–	–	–	–	–	–	–
Greece	2002		U	rural	–	–	–	–	↓	most ↑	↓	–	–	5
Hungary	1997	268	U	–	95%	–	–	5%	–	–	–	–	–	2
Iceland	2002		U, P	all	–	–	–	–	–	–	–	–	–	–
Ireland	2002	All domestic water charges have been consolidated into general taxation since 1 January 1997												
Italy	1998		P	–	–	–	–	–	–	100%	–	–	–	3-5
Japan	1998	1900	U	–	–	–	42%	–	–	57%	–	–	1%	2-7
Korea	1998		P, U	–	–	–	–	↓	100%	↑	–	–	–	6-10
Luxembourg	1997	118	U	–	↓	some	↑	↓	some	↑	↓	some	↑	2-3
Mexico	2002		U	–	–	–	–	↓	most	↑	↓	most	↑	6-7
N. Zealand	1998		P	75%	–	25%	–	–	–	–	–	–	–	–
Netherlands	1998	18	U	–	1	16	–	–	2	–	–	–	–	2
Norway	2002		P	87%	–	13%	–	–	–	–	–	–	–	–
Poland	1998		P, U	–	–	most	–	–	–	–	–	–	–	–

Table 3.2. Public water supply: household tariff structure
(% of utilities [U] or population [P] with a given structure) (cont.)

	Year	No. utilities in sample (and % of pop. represented)	Unit	Flat fee	CONSTANT VOLUMETRIC RATE			INCREASING-BLOCK SCHEDULE			DECREASING-BLOCK SCHEDULE			Normal number of blocks
					No fixed charge	Plus fixed charge	Plus fixed + min.	No fixed charge	Plus fixed charge	Plus fixed + min.	No fixed charge	Plus fixed charge	Plus fixed + min.	
Portugal	2002	23	U	–	–	–	–	–	23	–	–	–	–	3-5
Spain	2001	700	P (U)	–	↓	10% (<200)	↗	↓	85% (<500)	↗	↓	5% (15)	↗	2-5
Sweden	2000	288	U	–	–	100%	–	–	–	–	–	–	–	–
Switzerland	1998	all	P (U)	–	–	95% (235)	–	–	5% (1)	–	–	–	–	2
Turkey	1998	all	P	rural	–	–	–	↓	<100%	↗	–	–	–	3
UK	1998													
Eng. and Wales	2002	all (26)	P	77%	23%									–
Scotland	2000	all (3)	P	>99%	–	0.014%								–
N. Ireland	2002	all (1)	P	100%	All domestic charge met from general taxation									
US	2002	145	U	–%	1%	←35%		1%	←33%	↗	←	29%	↗	2-4

Australia: Tariff structure applies to year to 30 June 2001.
Austria: Raw tariff data for 71 municipalities was provided by Federal Ministry of the Environment.
Belgium: Tariff structures with free allowances per household or per capita designated as increasing block.
Canada: Figures refer to % of population sample (= 75% of national population) served by each tariff type.
France: Old survey data. Water Law of 1992 ruled out (minor exceptions) i) flat-fee and ii) const.vol.rate + fixed + min.charge, which are now in decline.
Germany: At most, 5% of utilities apply a linear tariff with no fixed element.
Italy: A very small fixed charge (meter rent) is applied, and often a free minimum allowance as well. The minimum charge, which constitutes the first (lowest-priced) block, charged at the basic rate, is being phased out over four years, from April 2001.
Japan: Water utilities levy a minimum charge but generally do not impose a separate fixed charge.
Netherlands: One utility (Wgron) offers domestic consumers a free allowance of 25 or 28 m3/year/household, and another (Brabant Water) gives household consumers in one of its four districts a free allowance of 15m3/year/household.
Portugal: Information applying to 23 larger water supply utilities.
United Kingdom: In all parts of the UK except Northern Ireland, a choice of domestic metering (and volumetric charging) is available to all households, except those living in new houses (which are generally metered when they are built) and i) users of garden sprinklers and swimming pools and ii) certain other selected groups of high-use houses or households are also compulsorily metered.
Apartments: There is no necessary consistency with the data embedded in Table 3.1, reflecting the tariff structures by which individual apartments and apartment buildings are charged in different countries. The best presumption is probably that the percentage figures refer, jointly, to single-family houses and apartment buildings. This is not uniformly true, however, in England and Wales, for example, the option of "free metering" (no installation cost is paid) extends to all individual apartment-dwellers.

Source: OECD (2003b).

Comprehensive Water Management Countermeasures led to the abandonment of minimum fixed charges by 59 of 167 local governments. Hungary, Poland, and the Czech Republic already use pricing systems based solely on volumetric pricing, with no fixed charge element at all.

Within the volumetric charge, the trend is away from decreasing-block tariffs and towards increasing-block ones, in which the charge increases with each additional unit of water used or wastewater treated. There are also some experiments with "peak pricing" arrangements, especially seasonal pricing, though little interest has so far been expressed in other forms of temporal variation, such as time-of-day pricing.

The price structures in place for public sewage-related services are not always clear, mainly because responsibility for sewerage, sewage treatment, and drainage is typically held by different bodies, each with its own principles and practices. However, available data suggest that sewage charges are usually directly related to volumes of water delivered from the public water supply system. Thus, the structure of wastewater charging systems tends to closely follow that of household water supply systems in most OECD countries, although the trend towards more incentive-based charging for the public water supply has generally led to more wastewater revenue being recovered through volumetric charging.

Direct abstraction from the environment represents roughly 75% of total water consumption by the industrial sector (on average) in OECD countries. As the public system is thus not the major source of industrial supply, it is difficult to generalise about price structures in the industrial sector as a whole.

Industrial water services connected to the public system are almost always metered. Most of these services are subject to two-part tariffs, involving fixed and volumetric components. The variable part can be either decreasing-block or increasing-block. Connection charges also exist in some countries (*e.g.* Denmark, France, and Finland). Industries often benefit from special contract arrangements related to their water services. Conversely, they sometimes are expected to contribute to special "one-off" investment costs (*e.g.* in Ireland and Hungary).

There is also movement towards marginal cost pricing in certain countries: some industrial groups in Germany face lower prices off-peak, and a degree of seasonal pricing for industrial users is employed in parts of the US and in France.

Since the volume and characteristics of industrial sewage vary considerably by company or plant, industrial water consumption levels are not a good proxy for industrial sewerage and sewage disposal costs. Recognition of this, along with a general shift towards more cost-reflective water tariffs for industry, has resulted in a trend towards separating water use charges from wastewater charges in industry. In only a few OECD countries today are the costs of industrial sewerage services still included in the price of water supply.

In most countries, standard sewerage charges are supplemented by "special strength" charges designed to recover the costs of any extra capacity that is required to treat particular industrial effluents. Some municipalities, however, do not use these charges, either because they are concerned about the competitiveness implications for local industry or because they perceive the monitoring costs as too high.

Industrial effluent charges usually depend on the metered volume of pollutants and/or pollution content. In France, for example, a charge is levied on the eight types of pollutant deemed most dangerous and difficult to treat (heavy metals, phosphorus, soluble salts, etc.). The charge is calculated as a function of pollution produced during the period of maximum activity on a normal day. In other cases, the charging formula can reflect the costs of treating a particular effluent, or the environmental sensitivity of the receiving waters.

Service providers generally receive the proceeds of industrial effluent charges. This revenue may be channelled into an investment fund that can either allocate the money to water service providers or commission wastewater treatment investments directly. In France, for example, industrial users discharging to the public sewers pay a pollution charge that varies according to the pollution load of the discharge. The service provider collects the charge through the water bill and pays it to the appropriate River Basin Agency.

In countries where sewerage service costs have risen significantly, industrial users are increasingly questioning whether discharging to the public sewer system is the most cost-effective approach, and there is evidence of a trend towards more self-treatment and effluent reuse.

About half of OECD countries levy general abstraction charges, usually on water abstracted outside the public system – most of which is industrial water – but sometimes also on public service providers. In many cases such charges are relatively recent (e.g. Germany 1985, the Netherlands 1995); in others they are much older. France, for instance, set up its River Basin Agencies in 1964, with a sophisticated regime of abstraction charges established at river basin level.

Abstraction charges typically vary by category of use, and often by location (in which case they sometimes reflect water scarcity). In some countries, the abstraction charge has an explicit environmental objective, so the proceeds are allocated to an environmental fund. The Netherlands has two abstraction charges, one levied by the provinces for groundwater protection, the other levied by the state within the general taxation regime. In Belgium, only industrial abstraction from groundwater are covered, the proceeds going to a special groundwater protection fund.

General discharge controls are also often imposed on direct wastewater discharges that do not go through the public sewer. The proceeds of these charges always go to the government, since there is no service provider involved. Most commonly, a permit is required for discharging directly back into a river or aquifer. Most OECD countries regulate the quality of waters into which discharges can be made.

There are variations on this theme, however. In the Netherlands, for example, it is only discharges from the largest polluters that are actually metered. For smaller polluters, pollution loads are estimated using input-output models for each industrial sector. In Mexico, dischargers can obtain *ex ante* discounts on their discharge fees if they can demonstrate that significant efforts have been made to pre-treat effluents. Similarly, in Germany, there is a 75% reduction in the basic charge if the standards contained in the regulations (expressed as "best available technique") are met.

Tariff levels

Practices among OECD countries concerning the imposition of water taxes and charges, both on piped household services and at other stages of the water cycle, vary widely. VAT is the most common type of tax. Other distinctive charges on water use are encountered, such as France's levy for the Fonds National des Adductions d'Eau. This charge, which adds about 1% to household water bills, provides funds for rural water and wastewater services, effectively financing some capital costs.

Though the principle of "full cost internalisation" (*i.e.* covering both investment or capital costs, operation and maintenance costs, and – in some cases – the costs of purchasing water rights) is becoming more widespread in the provision of water and wastewater services, current practice does not yet fully conform with this principle. For example, a considerable backlog of investment needs in wastewater treatment capacity remains unmet in several OECD countries.

Water supply subsidies also remain high. Such subsidies may reflect a perception that the resource is abundant or that the public good is always served by building water infrastructure. Furthermore, the history of government involvement in water service provision is deeply entrenched. In sum, municipalities face considerable political constraints in setting water charges at levels that reflect full costs.

This situation seems to be changing in many countries, however, with growing awareness that: i) water quality is often getting worse as a result of over-consumption (especially where groundwater is involved); ii) government budgets have been stretched to the limit and can no longer be counted on to maintain water infrastructure; and iii) more efficient and equitable approaches than across-the-board subsidies are available for achieving social (affordability) goals.

Table 3.3 shows the recent annual rates of change in water tariffs for 14 countries, in nominal and real terms. Scotland and the Czech Republic indicate untypically large annual real increases because they are transitional, at 16.1% and 14.8% a year respectively. The remaining 12 countries indicate rates of change of between –1.5% a year (Australia) and +5.0% a year (Denmark), with a simple, unweighted mean of 1.6%. This is significantly less than the 3.7% annual increase identified in earlier studies (OECD, 1999b). It suggests that, although the underlying trend remains upwards, governments may have begun to regulate price increases more carefully in recent years.

Table 3.3. **Summary of recent changes in household water tariffs**

	Years	Nominal (aggregate) increase	Average real (annual) increase
Australia	1996-00	0.2	–1.5
Austria (Vienna)	1992-99	5.7	3.8
Belgium (Brussels)	1988-98	5.1	2.7
Canada	1994-99	3.2	1.5
Czech Republic	1997-00	21.7	14.8
Denmark	1995-01	7.4	5.0
Finland	1997-02	3.1	1.1
France	1995-00	3.1	1.8
Germany	1995-01	2.4	0.8
Hungary	1997-02	12.1	2.1
Mexico	1997-01	10.1	–2.1
Sweden	1991-99	4.1	2.4
UK			
England and Wales	1994-01	1.2	–1.4
Scotland	1997-00	19.2	16.1
US	1997-01	2.9	0.4

Source: OECD (2003b).

Denmark, with one of the larger price increases indicated (5% annually), provides an interesting example of a country that has been trying to address its water quality (groundwater) problems via measures to reduce water demand. France experienced very large annual increases in household water charges (7%) during the first half of the 1990s, largely reflecting impending implementation of the European Union Waste Water Treatment Directive, but then significantly reduced its average annual real increases (to 1.8%). The Czech Republic and Hungary are examples of countries that have realised very large absolute reductions in subsidies in recent years.

The main factors contributing to these increases in water charges are as follows.

● Past pollution of groundwater continues to necessitate either more sophisticated and hence more expensive treatment, or abandonment of aquifers, with a consequent need to develop more expensive demand-management or supply-based regimes.

● Maintaining and enhancing existing sources can require more elaborate treatment to deal with new organic pollutants, often from non-point sources.

● Both national legislation and EU directives are requiring tighter wastewater treatment standards.

As these trends are unlikely to be significantly reversed in the near future, further price increases are on the short-term planning horizon for most OECD countries.

The water use that is subject to the lowest charges (and receives the highest subsidies) in most OECD countries is for irrigation purposes. In many countries, public bodies manage large collective irrigation networks and the price of water supplied to farmers rarely reflects its full social cost. Recent OECD reports indicate that industrial and household water users often pay more than 100 times as much as agricultural users (Figure 3.1). Some caution is required in drawing comparisons between water prices paid by different users, however, because water supplied to agriculture is usually of lower quality than that used by households, and the capital and running costs of water conveyance systems are generally lower for agriculture than for households or industry.

In countries where irrigation is relatively important, key variables include the type of water rights, pricing criteria, type of charges, and the performance and use of alternative economic instruments. In assessing the economic distortions that may be caused by under-pricing agricultural water, it is also important to take into account both the negative and positive effects of agricultural water use on the environment. Management of water resources for agricultural purposes can help prevent or contribute to flooding, and can filter or buffer rainwater or add contaminants to it as it passes through or across the soil. These effects may vary according to agro-ecosystems, farming systems, climatic conditions, and government policies.

Even with these caveats taken into account, however, it is clear that water prices are significantly lower for agriculture than for other user sectors in most OECD countries. A number of OECD countries, however, are beginning to embark on major reforms that are intended to help change this situation (see Box 2.2 above).

Figure 3.1.   **Comparison of agricultural, industrial, and household water prices (late 1990s)**

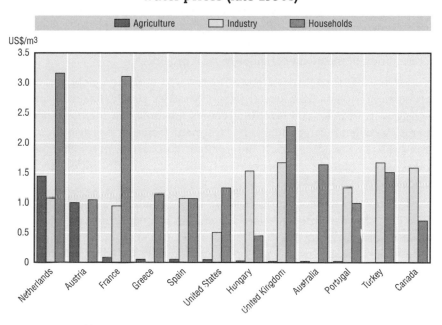

Source: OECD (2001b).

Water infrastructure subsidies

Historically, public expenditure on water infrastructure in most countries has been financed through the tax system. This practice is becoming difficult to sustain, partly because tax revenues are increasingly insufficient to meet all competing needs (e.g. social welfare programmes, health systems, defence). It is therefore crucial that available funds be used to the greatest possible effect.

Subsidies to the water sector take a variety of forms, including capital subsidies, operating transfers (which serve to keep average tariffs below the full economic costs of provision), and cross-subsidies (which involve differentiating tariffs across customer groups). The result is that water consumers frequently do not pay the full cost of the water they use. And since subsidies can be volatile, water utilities often do not have sufficient funds to maintain and operate the water infrastructure already in place.

Although often justified in terms of keeping services affordable to poor households, subsidies are seldom well targeted, and therefore not very effective. Instead of benefiting the poor, who may not even be connected to water distribution and sanitation networks, subsidies often go to middle-income groups that are generally considered capable of paying the full costs of water services. The effectiveness of public spending on water infrastructure could be increased if subsidies were restructured and better targeted. Provided that the poor are adequately protected, wider application of the user pays principle would help put utility financing on a more sustainable basis and would slow the deterioration of urban water infrastructure (as well as deterioration in the quality of the services it provides).

Several OECD countries are moving towards more complete recovery of infrastructure costs from users, although rather slowly. Recovery implies setting water prices at a level that covers not only the maintenance and operating costs of water supply and treatment facilities, but also their long-term capital costs. More broadly interpreted, "full cost recovery charging" for water infrastructure also generates funds for essential pipe repair and replacement.

Greater transparency in the level of implicit subsidies (including cross-subsidies) provided through undercharging for infrastructure use could help build up momentum for further reforms. So would involving other stakeholders (*e.g.* the private sector and community-based organisations) in key investment and management decisions associated with water infrastructure.

Social issues in the pricing of water services

Affordability

Affordability can be most easily thought of as the prevailing level of water service charges in relation to the disposable income of consumers. The affordability of a given water service may not be distributed equitably among income groups or neighbourhoods. For the same water consumption level and total bill, a poorer household will inevitably pay a higher proportion of its income than a higher-income household (this is the "micro" aspect of affordability). If the poorer household happens to be in a new housing development, its water prices could be higher than those in a richer but older neighbourhood nearby, because of capital cost recovery requirements for service expansion (OECD, 2003b).

"Aggregate (or macro)" affordability for a country is measured by relating average household water charges to either average household income or average household aggregate expenditure. Table 3.4 brings together some macro affordability measurements for selected OECD countries.

On average, water tariffs at the national level typically amount to less than 2% of disposable income for OECD households. However, more detailed information on the full income distribution in eight OECD countries (Table 3.5) reveals larger burdens for particular lower-income groups: ranging from more

60

Table 3.4. **Recent macro affordability measurements**

	Year	Denominator (all refer to households)	PWS	S&ST	Water charges (proportion of income or expenditure)
Poland	1999	Disposable Y			2.2%/2.4%
Hungary	2000	Net Income	1.4%	0.7%	2.1%
Turkey	1997	"Income"			1.2-1.7%
Portugal	1997	"Income"			1.6%
Luxembourg	1997	"Income"			1.0-1.5%
Netherlands	1999	Disposable Y	0.6%	0.8%	1.4%
Mexico	2000	Disposable Y	1.3%		
Austria	1997	"Income"			1.0-1.3%
Germany	2000	Disposable Y	0.5%	0.7%	1.2%
England and Wales	1997-00	Disposable Y			1.2%
Denmark	1998	Disposable Y	0.5%	0.6%	1.1%
France	1995	"Income"			0.9%
Slovak Rep.	2001	Net Income			0.9%
Scotland	1997-00	Disposable Y			0.7%
Japan	2000	Expenditure			0.7%
Italy	1997	Expenditure			0.7%
Korea	1997-98	Expenditure			0.6%
United States	2000	Disposable Y			0.5%

PWS = public water supply; S&ST = sewerage and sewage treatment.
Source: OECD (2003b).

Table 3.5. **Comparison of water charge burdens**

	Year	Percentiles or number of classes	Disposable income as a basis for measurement of water charge burden	
			Burden of lowest income group	Ratio of lowest income group burden to average burden
England and Wales	1999-00	Deciles	3.75%[1]	3.1[2]
Mexico[3]	2000	Deciles	3.84%	3.0
Hungary	1999	Deciles	2.53%	1.4
Scotland	1999-00	Deciles	2.24%[1]	< 2.9
France[4]	1995	Nine	2.18%	2.5
Netherlands	1999	Quartiles	2.38%	1.7
Denmark	1998	Six	1.93%	1.7
Italy	1995	Six	0.90%[5]	> 2.1
United States[6]	2000	Quintiles	0.66%	1.3

1. Average gross and average net incomes for the lowest income group are assumed to be equal.
2. Separate data provided by the UK Office of National Statistics enabled this figure to be estimated directly.
3. Data are believed to refer only to public water supply.
4. "Income" measures used in the sample survey are assumed to refer to disposable income.
5. For the lowest income groups total expenditure is assumed to equal net income.
6. Communications with the Federal Bureau of Labour Statistics led to an assumption that in the case of the two lowest income quintiles the reporting of incomes was so incomplete that total average household expenditure for those groups would be a better guide to average disposable income.
Source: OECD (2003b).

than 3% (England and Wales, and Mexico), to between 2 and 3% (Scotland, France, Hungary, and the Netherlands).[1]

Figure 3.2 summarises the whole range of social policy measures being used by OECD countries to make water services more affordable for lower-income households. Such policy measures can be classified into two main types, *income support measures* and *tariff-related measures*. The former includes those addressing the individual customer's affordability problem from the income side, through absolute-value water bill reductions or waivers (*e.g.* income assistance, water vouchers, tariff rebates and discounts, arreas forgiveness). Tariff-related measures seek to reduce low-income customers' bills by restricting price and aiming to reduce consumption (*e.g.* social tariffs through cross-subsidisation targetted at designed groups, capping of metered tariffs for low-income consumers).

Improving access of the urban poor to basic water and sanitation services

Special efforts are needed to provide access to water for the urban poor and ensure that they can afford water services, while still maintaining incentives for efficient water use. This implies making maximum use of low-cost options and involving communities directly in the service provision. Box 3.1 summarises some of the issues and opportunities.

Figure 3.2. **Policy measures dealing with affordability**

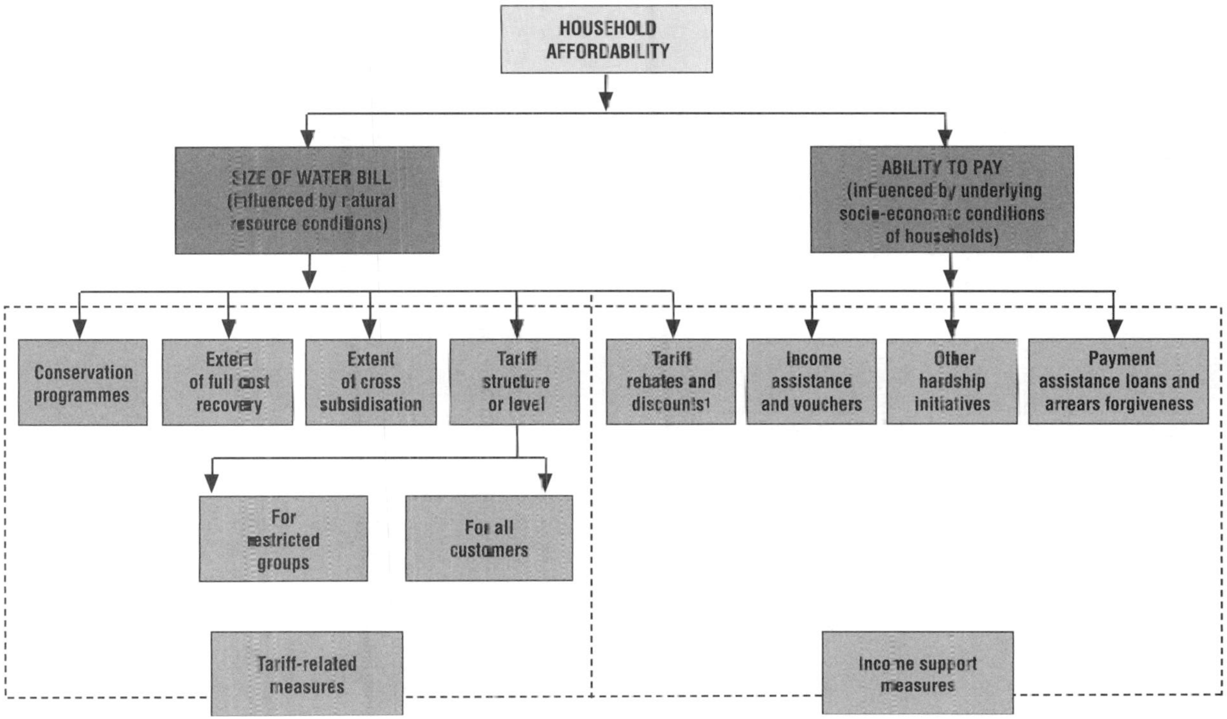

1. Tariff rebates and discounts are included in the "Income Support Measures" box since in the majority of cases they are fixed in advance and thus not subject to variation due to changes in consumption behaviour. Since their effect is thus to increase disposable income, they have most in common with income-support measures.

Box 3.1. **Issues in improving access to affordable water services for the urban poor**

Technical issues: These include the cost of supply, which depends on a settlement's distance from existing water mains, sewers, and drains; the topography, soil structure, settlement density and layout; and the potential for tapping local water resources.

Institutional issues: These include the attitude of the authorities with regard to the provision of water and sanitation in shantytowns and unauthorised settlements, as well as the status of the residents, (*i.e.* whether they are "owners" or "tenants"). It is difficult for water utilities to provide connections (and receive regular payments) where it is not clear who owns what land, or where houses have no official addresses.

Demand factors: Detailed information on existing (formal and informal) water and sanitation systems is essential. It should include analysis of residents' needs and their ability/willingness to pay. If communities have secured sufficient access to water through informal means, they may have other priorities than the upgrading of those systems.

Differentiated services: Where it is too expensive to provide piped water to each household, other options can be considered. For example, the water agency can provide connections to water mains and trunk sewers at the settlement's boundary, with the inhabitants organising the system within the settlement. The agency thus "wholesales" water to a community, which in turn assumes responsibility for collecting payment from households. (By installing a community water meter, the agency avoids the costs of providing and monitoring individual house meters.)

Partial self-provision: The costs of installing pipes for water and/or sanitation can be considerably reduced if household and/or community organisations are prepared to dig the ditches and to ensure that houses are prepared for connection. Using smaller pipes and shallower trenches, shallower gradients and interceptor tanks can also reduce the cost of installing sewerage systems, though changes in demand over the longer term should be kept in mind if this approach is taken.

Sewer-less sanitation: Many low-cost options also exist for safe sewer-less sanitation (*e.g.* ventilated improved pit latrines or pour-flush toilets linked to community septic tanks) However, such facilities require regular emptying and disposal.

Payment procedures: Access to water and sanitation can be facilitated by allowing the initial connection charges to be paid over time or through loan arrangements.

Source: OECD (2003b).

Note

1. Different methodologies exist for measuring the burden of water charges on household incomes. Some measure the average household water charge relative to the disposable income, others measure it relative to gross household income or to aggregate expenditure. It seems most appropriate, wherever possible, to relate charges to disposable income (as used in Table 3.5), since it most closely reflects household budget constraints.

ISBN 92-64-09948-4
Improving Water Management
Recent OECD Experience
© OECD 2003

Chapter 4

Water Pricing in Selected Non-OECD Countries[1]

Water pricing

In the countries of the former Soviet Union now known collectively as EECCA (Eastern Europe, Caucasus, and Central Asia[2]), 80% or more of the urban population is connected to the public water supply, and more than 60% to public sewer systems. This rather extensive infrastructure is rapidly deteriorating, however, resulting in reduced service quality and increased health and environmental risks. In some countries, more than one-third of the population is using drinking water that does not meet basic hygiene standards; in some sub-regions the proportion can exceed 50% (OECD, 2003a forthcoming). Unlike the situation in much of the developing world, therefore, the challenge here in achieving the Millennium Development Goals related to water lies not in extending networks, but in maintaining them.[3]

Following the rapid decentralisation of responsibility for water management from central to municipal level, it is now common in most EECCA countries for urban water and sanitation systems to be managed by municipal or district water companies owned by local authorities. The rapid removal of state subsidies in the 1990s in the process of decentralisation (except in Turkmenistan), and the inability to compensate through municipal budgets and tariffs, resulted in serious under-funding of water infrastructure. Water services are now provided at prices well below long-run financial and environmental costs, resulting in water overuse and wastage.

Household water use in the EECCA countries is relatively high – between 200 litres per capita a day (lpcd) in small towns and 500 lpcd in large cities – despite significant decreases in some countries (*e.g.* Moldova). Consumption levels appear to be even higher in certain locations, such as Tbilisi, Georgia (up to 900 lpcd), and Ashgabat, Turkmenistan (700 lpcd). One reason the apparent consumption is so high is that metering is not yet widely used so there is little incentive for more efficient use. Furthermore, consumption data probably include a substantial amount of water that is lost in the distribution network through leakage.

Water metering (especially in apartment buildings) is only gradually being applied. In the Russian Federation and Ukraine, fewer than 30% of connections are metered; by comparison, the proportion is as much as 100% in some OECD and Baltic countries. Even where installed, water meters are not always used for billing purposes; in Almaty, Chisinau, and many other relatively large cities, for instance, utilities sign contracts not with individual consumers but with associations of apartment owners or housing maintenance companies.

Table 4.1 shows the current situation in the EECCA countries. Recovery levels for operating and maintenance costs from household consumers are frequently less than 50%. In some parts of the Caucasus, cost recovery levels can be as low as 20%. Industrial water tariffs are frequently much higher, since the Soviet system involved cross-subsidisation of household consumers. It is not uncommon for industry to pay five times as much as households, though the differences are now being reduced, and some countries (*e.g.* Kazakhstan) have undertaken to abolish cross-subsidisation.

Table 4.1.   **Comparative analysis of tariff policies for water supply in the EECCA**

	Cost recovery level from households (%)	Cross-subsidy ratio/presence	Full-cost-recovery target date
Armenia	20	5	2005
Azerbaijan	20-57	5[1]	2005
Belarus	31	48.6	2005 (80%)[2]
Georgia	15	yes	2005
Kazakhstan	100	no	1998
Kyrgyz Rep.	48	yes	2005 (75%)[3]
Moldova	50	yes	2003
Russia	60	4	2003
Turkmenistan	0	no	no
Ukraine	73[4]	yes	2005
Uzbekistan	100	no	2001

1. Data are for Yerevan only.
2. The Belarus target is to recover 80% of costs from households by 2005.
3. The Kyrgyz Republic target is to recover 75% of costs by 2005.
4. The figure represents the collection rate; nine out of 27 regions in Ukraine have reached 100% cost recovery for households.
Source: OECD (2003a forthcoming).

The lack of revenue available to water utilities is typically exacerbated by dramatically low collection rates from consumers. For example, in Azerbaijan, collection rates rarely exceed 70%, despite aid-funded efforts to improve the situation (World Bank, 2000); and in many cities, the situation is worse. This problem, combined with poor management practices, severely undermines the ability of water utilities to maintain, let alone expand or upgrade, their infrastructure networks.

Water utilities have been reacting to the lack of funding by delaying crucial maintenance work, closing certain wastewater treatment facilities, and sometimes reducing water services' availability to as little as two hours a day. In Yerevan, Armenia, for example, water is supplied for between two and six hours a day (UNECE, 2000).

While the financial situation could be significantly improved by increasing collection rates and decreasing production costs (*e.g.* by reducing leakage, improving energy efficiency, and adjusting staffing levels), some tariff increases are probably inevitable. Most EECCA governments have adopted full cost recovery as a medium-term objective (2005) and have developed schedules for achieving that objective. However, implementation has been slow, and progress to date mostly unsatisfactory.

In short, the EECCA countries have seen a very rapid increase in water prices over the past decade (*e.g.* from less than 4% to 100% recovery of operating costs in parts of Ukraine), and this trend is likely to continue. Even after full recovery is achieved for operation and maintenance costs associated with the present infrastructure, further upward pressures on water tariffs can be expected, especially since the need to improve wastewater treatment infrastructure will grow in political importance in some countries.

Infrastructure financing

Investment in the water sector has been very low in most EECCA countries, largely due to utilities' difficult revenue situations and the scarcity of public funds. Utility performance data for the Russian Federation indicate that about half of utilities surveyed did not invest at all between 1997-2001, and the other half either could not provide information or invested less than USD 0.10 per capita served per year. This means that not only have services not been extended or upgraded, but hardly any rehabilitation has been done. In Moldova, the situation is somewhat better, if still at very low levels, with investment in the range of USD 1.80 to 2.70 per capita – largely thanks to loans provided in projects by donors and international financial institutions. (For comparison, investment per capita in the Baltic states was about USD 40 per year in 1995-96[4]).

This situation stands in stark contrast with actual investment needs in EECCA and further underlines the challenges posed by continued infrastructure deterioration. For instance, data collected for finance strategy planning for the Kazakh urban water sector indicate that half of the supply networks, more than one-fourth of the sewerage networks, and close to one-third of the wastewater treatment plants need rehabilitation (OECD-DANCEE, 2001a). Kazakhstan needs to spend the equivalent of USD 230.5 million a year just to operate and maintain the infrastructure in its present (unsatisfactory) condition. This represents about 10% of annual average per capita income in households. The Kazakh finance strategy shows that to meet the financial

Box 4.1. **Applying environmental financing strategies in China**

Environmental Financing Strategy is a standardised methodological framework, supported by a specialised software application called *FEASIBLE©*, to help prepare realistic, multi-year action programmes for environmental sectors that require heavy capital investments in public infrastructure. FEASIBLE© calculates the investment, maintenance, and operation expenditure needed to reach targets set by local policy makers. The result is then compared with expected levels and sources of finance to help policy-makers understand where the main bottlenecks are and what policy intervention is needed to facilitate effective financing of infrastructure development programmes. To date, financing strategies have been prepared for the urban water and wastewater sector in Georgia, Moldova, Ukraine, and Kazakhstan, and for Novgorod and Pskov Oblasts in the Russian Federation.

The *FEASIBLE©* model is being applied to 14 cities and urban zones in the Sichuan Province of China with a total population of 3 million people. The baseline scenario for this exercise reflects the assumption that status quo trends that existed in 2000 will continue until 2020. Under this scenario, the following conclusions were made:

● Investment needs are several times higher for wastewater collection systems than for wastewater treatment plants.

● Sewer system development will lag behind wastewater treatment plant construction, so that by 2004, new treatment plants will not have enough wastewater.

● The structure of finance sourcing relies much more heavily on public budgets (rather than user fees) than in OECD countries.

● Wastewater fees paid by households, industry, and other consumers cover only about 30% of infrastructure operating costs and less than 20% of operation and maintenance combined.

● Domestic sources of finance (user fees and public budgets) could cover the operating and maintenance costs.

● On average, the current water and wastewater tariffs are affordable, but in most cities the poorest 10-20% of the population will need additional social support.

In a second phase of work, the OECD is working with the Chinese government to simulate how the baseline scenario could be altered through the application of different policy instruments.

Source: OECD (2003b forthcoming).

needs without increasing tariffs beyond affordability levels,[5] public spending on the water sector would gradually have to rise until it is 20 times the present level, even with substantial foreign investment and donor assistance.

In Georgia, the equivalent of USD 81.5 million a year is needed to maintain infrastructure in its present (unsatisfactory) condition.[6] This represents about 7% of annual per capita income in households in the capital, Tbilisi, and 11% in rural areas. Even assuming that this financial need is met, including significant donor and loan support, and that appropriate maintenance is carried out, most of the water system will continue to deteriorate in the short and medium term. In this scenario, it will be possible to restore 1999 service levels and quality of service only after 20 years. More ambitious development targets will only be realisable locally, since Georgia is unlikely to be able to afford rehabilitation on a nation-wide scale (OECD-DANCEE, 2001b).

While the financing strategies developed by the OECD and Denmark for several EECCA countries assumed that obstacles to sector investment and tariff adjustment would be removed, this is far from the case. Many country-specific issues hinder the development of water projects. For example, Russian law limits access to information on network and water intake for cities with populations above 1 million. Ukrainian municipalities with populations below 500 000 cannot obtain sovereign guarantees over their water infrastructure. In Kazakhstan, regional anti-monopoly committees (not the municipalities) approve tariffs and the national water agency approves water intake permits and water utility charters. In small countries such as the Kyrgyz Republic, Moldova, and those in the Caucasus, national bodies must approve tariff-related decisions and utility restructuring.

As a consequence, flows of ODA to EECCA have been slow. While most donors regard water supply and wastewater treatment as priority areas for their environmental co-operation activities in EECCA countries (Project Preparation Committee, 2002), bilateral environmental assistance to the region is still relatively small. International financial institutions have undertaken few water projects in EECCA countries; many planned projects have been cancelled, and only a few remain in the pipeline.

Social issues

Affordability

Political resistance to increasing water prices is high in the EECCA countries, and presents a serious obstacle to reform. Water services were traditionally considered social services and were provided at very low prices. Consumers have problems accepting the rapid increase in prices for deteriorating services. In Ukraine, for example, over 1992-2001 water prices rose about 16 times faster than prices for other goods and services, while the quality of drinking water and of water services visibly declined. EECCA country investments in water supply and sanitation services as a percentage of GDP are comparable with, and in some cases higher than, the investments in OECD countries (OECD, 2003a forthcoming). This suggests that it is low "ability to pay", rather than low "willingness to pay", that is the main obstacle.

Most consumers would be willing to pay more for better water quality and improved reliability. For example, willingness to pay (WTP) studies carried out in Lutsk, Ukraine, showed that 22% of households would be prepared to accept a 10% tariff increase (Romanyuk and Sarioglo, 2002). It should be noted, however, that willingness to pay is not the same among all groups of consumers: it is generally higher in families with higher levels of income and with children, and lower among retired people.

Subjective opinions of householders, which can be revealed through WTP studies, need to be supplemented by analysis of economic affordability using more objective statistical data about household income and expenses for water and other goods and services. OECD compared current water prices with household expenses in EECCA (OECD, 2003a forthcoming). The results demonstrate that even at the present low cost-recovery ratios, the average or macro affordability figures are equal to, or higher than, those in the OECD (Table 4.2).

Table 4.2.   **Macro affordability in selected EECCA countries (2001)**

	Expenses for water supply and sanitation services, USD/household/month	Total income/expenses of households, USD/month	Share of water supply and sanitation services in the income/expenses of households, %		
			Water supply	Sanitation	Total
Armenia	2.20	112.51 income	1.74	0.22	1.96
Belarus	0.85	138.10 income	0.37	0.24	0.62
Georgia	2.51	126.77 income	1.93	0.05	1.98
Russia	4.45	223.15 income	1.06	0.94	1.99
Uzbekistan	2.68	116.20 income	1.14	1.17	2.31
Ukraine	3.47	113.04 expenses	1.86	1.22	3.07
Kyrgyz Rep.	1.02	66.83 income	1.10	0.43	1.52
Poland (1999)		disposable income			2.3
Germany (2000)		disposable income			1.2
US (2002)		disposable income			0.5

Source: OECD (2003a forthcoming).

Macro affordability figures should be treated with caution, as they hide many essential differences among income groups and local conditions. For example, in Armenia, where the level of cost recovery is 20%, at current prices

9.7% of households already pay more than 4% of their total expenses for water and sanitation services; in the Kyrgyz Republic, 48% of costs are recovered and 18.5% of households pay above 4% at current prices (Figure 4.1).

Figure 4.1. **Water supply and sanitation price as share of household expense (% of households by size of share, 2001)**

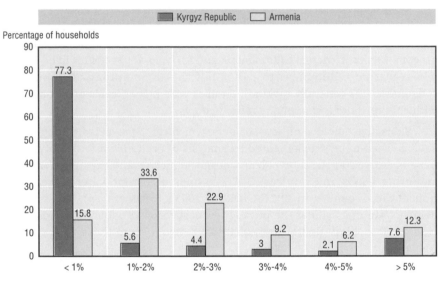

Source: OECD (2003a forthcoming).

Micro affordability analysis for Khmelnitski, Ukraine, shows that, at current prices and with 79% cost recovery, 22% of households pay more than 4% of their income for water services. If the price of water were to rise by 50%,[7] the share of such households would reach 43% (Figure 4.2).

Social assistance

In the past, EECCA countries used several mechanisms to assure access to water: i) general public subsidies to water utilities; ii) cross-subsidies for households via industrial tariffs; and iii) reduced or zero tariffs for "privileged" consumers, such as war veterans.

Facing serious public budget deficits, most EECCA governments (except Turkmenistan) have increasingly decided to move away from the financing of water supply and sanitation from public budgets and towards financing by water users. For example, in Ukraine the share of public financing of housing and communal services (including water) fell from 4.4% of GDP in 1994 to 0.6% in 2000. (In Russia, by comparison, total public financing for the sector

Figure 4.2. **Water supply and sanitation price as share of household expense in Khmelnitski (% of households by size of share)**

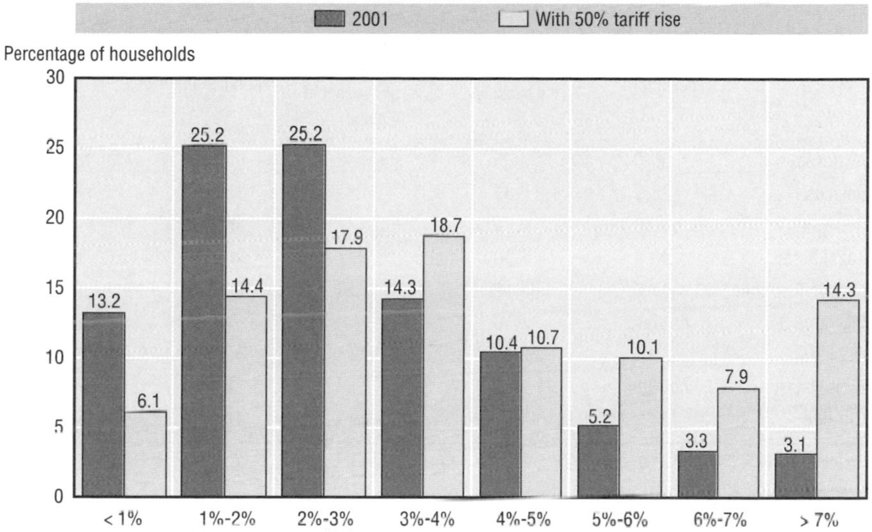

Source: OECD (2003a forthcoming).

remained around 7% of GDP in 2002.) Similarly, cross-subsidies are slowly being reduced, and in some countries (e.g. Kazakhstan), formally abolished.

Governments have had to replace across the board subsidies for all users with targeted subsidies for those who would not otherwise be able to afford their increased water bills (Table 4.3). Ukraine, Russia, and Kazakhstan have established housing subsidy programmes in which the central government provides compensation for household expenditures for housing and communal services (including water) that exceed a certain level of household income (20% in Ukraine, 22% in Russia, and 30% in Kazakhstan). In 2001, 11% of households in Ukraine received this housing subsidy in summer and 17% in winter. Equivalent to USD 100 per year on average, the subsidy represented 36.5% of total income for retired people and single-parent families. Such subsidies, provided as means-tested income support, allow significant savings for public budgets by channelling support to those who really need it. They also helped assure utility revenue during periods of rapid price increases by reducing non-payment.

Armenia and Uzbekistan (and, more recently, Ukraine) have means-tested income support programmes for families, which aim to increase income levels in general but do not target water or other communal services specifically. Such general poverty reduction programmes are a better

Table 4.3. **Selected social assistance programmes related to water, selected EECCA countries (2001)**

	% of poor in the population (national definition)	Housing Subsidy Programme		Privileges (share of recipients as % of total population)	Poverty reduction programme
		% of households receiving the subsidy	Maximum expenses for housing and communal services, as % of household income		
Armenia	50.9	0		0.86	yes
Belarus	28.9	0.81	15	15.89	no
Georgia	51.10	0		no data	no
Kazakhstan	28.4	7.50	30	no data	no
Kyrgyz Republic	47.6	45.10	25	no data	no
Moldova	no data	0		7.10	no
Russia	29.1	9.10	22	33.01	no
Uzbekistan	no data	0		3.51	yes
Ukraine	27.2	13.03	15-20	14.00	yes

Source: OECD (2003a forthcoming).

alternative to housing subsidies when the water bill is not significant in household expenses, but may be insufficient when a major water tariff reform is planned.

Most EECCA countries still provide subsidies through a system of privileges that grants discounted or free services to certain categories of citizen (*e.g.* police, judges, war veterans). These programmes do not target the poor and cannot be justified economically, but there is political resistance to removing them. Only in Moldova and Armenia have some of these privileges been eliminated.

Means-tested income support is one of the most effective and efficient tools for social support to the poor. In OECD countries, tariff-based measures are often used in addition to (or sometimes instead of) income subsidies. Such measures include "lifeline" and increasing-block tariffs to promote lower water consumption and thereby lower water bills. No use of tariff-based measures has been observed so far in EECCA countries, mainly because there is so little individual metering.

In addition to economic mechanisms to ensure that the poor have sufficient water, technical and legal policies can be used at both national and local level. These include alternative water supply, disconnection policies, and arrears management. In most EECCA countries, water service customers can in theory be disconnected for non-payment, though in practice this rarely happens because of technical difficulties and political opposition. Since there is such a high level of non-payment, however, arrears management measures, such as debt restructuring and forgiveness, are commonly used. While debt restructuring can be an effective tool, debt forgiveness has certain limitations as a policy option.

Depending on growth in household income, the affordability situation is likely to deteriorate significantly in a number of EECCA countries as utility reforms progress. Making these reforms socially acceptable will probably necessitate additional spending from already stretched public budgets, and it is not clear where this money will come from.

Public involvement

Where there is a "crisis of trust" between water users and water producers, poor information provision is among the main reasons. Local governments and utilities in EECCA countries seldom study consumer opinion and preferences. Consumers often do not know about measures planned for the sector. Furthermore, they seldom know how much water they use or what the real costs of water services are. There is a clear need to improve basic information about water quality, methods of additional water treatment, hygiene, and the potential for water conservation.

Public and consumer participation in decision making remains a controversial issue. Some consumer groups and NGOs believe they should have the right to participate directly in all decisions in the sector, including tariff setting and the degree of private-sector participation. While such an extreme interpretation of the right to participation would probably result in inefficient sector management, key areas of decision making do need to become much more transparent in many countries. Public access to information on decision making has been improved in a few cases in recent years, however. Ukraine's new law on drinking water, for example, provides a legal basis for public hearings on key issues in sector reforms. Kazakhstan's Antimonopoly Committee organises public hearings in cities and towns where tariff reforms could raise public concern.

Another reason for the "crisis of trust" between consumers and utilities lies in the unclear legal and institutional framework for service provision and difficulties in resolving conflicts. Individual households do not have direct contractual relations with water utilities, but interact with a housing maintenance agency or other intermediary service provider that has no incentive to assure the quality and efficiency of services. Quality parameters for water services are not clearly identified, are not well known to consumers, or are difficult to verify. Court procedures are too complicated for resolving disputes between water consumers and providers, and other methods have not yet been developed.

EECCA countries are working to address these problems. In Ukraine, for example, a model contract between consumers and providers was developed, but has proved difficult to implement. Some countries have sought to develop associations of apartment owners as legal entities representing consumers *vis-à-vis* water and other utilities. Certain utilities have improved their customer relations units and launched telephone hotlines; in some cases, consumers have received detailed bills with information about consumption and price. NGOs active in water campaigns work to educate consumers about water quality and conservation.

Notes

1. Most water pricing work being done by the OECD in non-OECD countries concerns Eastern Europe, the Caucasus, and Central Asia, although there has been a recent expansion to analyse water problems in other countries, such as China (see Box 4.1).

2. Armenia, Azerbaijan, Belarus, Georgia, Kazakhstan, Kyrgyz Republic, Moldova, Russian Federation, Tajikistan, Turkmenistan, Ukraine, and Uzbekistan.

3. These issues were addresses in a conference of Ministers of Environment, Finance, and Economics of the EECCA region (Almaty, October 2000). Ministers recognised the critical situation of water infrastructure, and adopted Guiding Principles for the Reform of the Urban Water Supply and Sanitation Sector in EECCA. The OECD-EAP Task Force was invited to develop a work programme to support and monitor implementation of these Guiding Principles.

4. See *www.water.hut.fi/bench/baltics.html#Indicator*

5. The affordability limit was assumed to be 4% of household income.

6. Characterised by frequent absence of proper chlorination, generally low pressure, frequent interruptions in drinking water supply, insufficient maintenance of water supply and sewerage systems.

7. A 50% increase, despite a cost recovery rate of 79%, assumes overestimation of the actual cost recovery level, and the need to phase out cross-subsidies between household and industrial consumers.

PART III

Improving Decision Making

Introduction

The management of freshwater resources involves a wide range of policy goals, only some of which will be complementary. For example, affordable and equitable access by all to safe drinking water and adequate sanitation may not always be compatible with local environmental constraints on the availability of water. To ensure the right mix of objectives, strong and coherent decision-making processes and institutions are needed.

To this end, OECD countries have been making significant changes in the institutional and management structures of their water service providers. For example, rather than leaving responsibility for water supply and wastewater treatment fragmented among numerous federal, state, and local bodies, many countries have adopted more integrated approaches. As the needs of ecosystems for regular minimum water flows become more apparent, countries are increasingly balancing social and economic water needs against an ecosystem approach.

Water resources are usually managed on the basis of political boundaries, even though they often cross political borders (two-thirds of the world's major catchment areas cross national boundaries). In some cases, conflicts occur between upstream users (who claim sovereign rights to water that originates or flows through their territory) and downstream users (who demand that given flow and water quality levels be maintained). Many treaties and other arrangements have therefore been drawn up to co-operatively manage cross-boundary basins.

Even within individual countries, different local political constituencies often share management of a basin. To avoid problems, countries are increasingly adopting a "whole-basin" approach to water management, setting up water supply and wastewater management institutions that reflect the geographic boundaries of river basins rather than political boundaries.

Another change being seen in many OECD countries is a move away from government as "provider" and more towards government as "regulator" of water services. This shift is often accompanied by increased public-private collaboration. There is a growing realisation that, under the right circumstances, such co-operation can lead to environmentally sustainable, economically efficient, and socially acceptable results. Chapter 5 highlights some of the main lessons learned through recent OECD work on institutional structures for water service management.

ISBN 92-64-09948-4
Improving Water Management
Recent OECD Experience
© OECD 2003

Chapter 5

Working in Partnership with the Private Sector

Basic reforms

Responsibility for water and sanitation services may rest at municipal, regional, or central government level. Many countries have recently undergone water sector reform, and it has become more common to separate the water provider institutionally from other arms of government by setting up "parastatals" or state-owned enterprises. By introducing some degree of institutional independence and financial incentive, considerable improvements in service efficiency have been made (Johnstone and Wood, 2001). Many have engaged the private sector in water services provision, utilising various institutional approaches from fully public water management to fully private (Figure 5.1). While discussions about private sector participation in the water

Figure 5.1.   **Basic modes of water sector organisation**

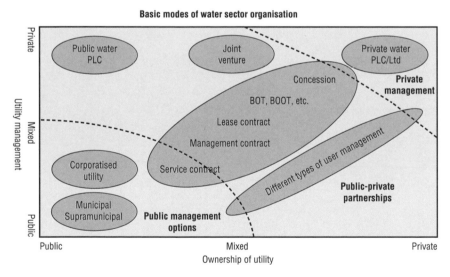

Basic modes of water sector organisation

Source: Blokland (2000).

sector often concentrate on full divestiture, which includes the transfer of asset ownership and responsibility for its management, there are in fact many other forms. A common point of all of these options is that the government always retains responsibility for setting and enforcing performance standards – regardless of the form of private involvement chosen.

Table 5.1. **Institutional arrangements in OECD countries**

	Public Supply	Ownership[1]	Management	Economic Regulator	Environmental Regulator
Australia	Regional/Municipal	Both	Both	Regional/indepen.	Provincial govts.
Austria	Municipal	Public	Public	Municipal	Central govt.
Belgium	Intermunicipal	Both	Both	Federal govt. (prices)	Regional
Canada	Regional	Public	Public	Provincial govt.	Provincial govt.
Czech Republic	Municipal	Private	Both	Central govt.	Central govt.
Denmark	Municipal	Public	Public	Municipal	Central govt./ municipalities
Finland	Municipal	Public	Public	Municipal	Central govt.
France	Municipal	Public	Both	Municipal	Central govt.
Germany	Inter-municipal/ Municipal/Regional	Both	Both	Municipal/Region	Regional
Greece	Municipal	Public	Public	Central govt.	Central govt.
Hungary	Municipal	Public	Both	Central govt.	Central govt./ Independent
Iceland	Municipal	n.a.	n.a.	n.a.	Central govt.
Ireland	Regional	Public	Public	Regional	Central govt.
Italy	Municipal	Public	Public[2]	Central and region. govts.	Central and regional govts.
Japan	Municipal	Public	Public[2]	Central govt.	Central govt.
Korea	National/Regional	Public	Public	Central govt./regional	Central govt.
Luxembourg	Municipal	Public	Public	Municipal	n.a.
Mexico	Municipal	Public	Both	Central govt.	n.a.
Netherlands	Municipal	Public	Both	Central govt./regional	Central govt./regional
New Zealand	Municipal/Regional	Public	Both	Central govt.	Central govt.
Norway	Municipal	Both	Both	Central govt.	n.a.
Poland	Municipal	Public	Public	Municipal	Municipal
Portugal	Municipal/Regional	Public	Both	Central govt.	Central govt.
Spain	Municipal	Public	Both	Central govt.	Central govt./ independent
Sweden	Municipal	Public	Public	Municipal	Regional
Switzerland	Municipal	Public	Public	Central govt.	n.a.
Turkey	Municipal	Public	Public	Central govt.	Central govt./ Regional
United Kingdom (England and Wales)	Regional	Private	Private	Independent	Independent
United States	Municipal	Both	Both	Independent	Independent

n.a. not available.
1. "Both" means public and private ownership structures co-exist.
2. Private management exists but is marginal.
Source: Adapted from OECD (1999b).

OECD countries have generally been moving away from the "fully public" model for the water sector in recent years. The government role in water management has also been shifting from that of primary service provider to one of establishing and regulating an operating environment in which communities, the private sector, and NGOs become more active in the process of providing water and sanitation services. In several countries, independent economic regulators have been set up to regulate water prices autonomously. These regulators usually set prices and may have other responsibilities such as establishing service performance standards. Table 5.1 summarises the current situation.

Water supply systems remain largely publicly owned, mainly because of their natural monopoly characteristics. Yet service management is increasingly being delegated to private operators. This approach seems particularly well suited to decentralised systems where municipalities see delegation as a way to overcome their own lack of technical expertise or financial resources. In several countries, service providers can decide whether they want to manage the service themselves (direct management) or to delegate responsibility to a private operator via concessions (OECD, 1999b).

It is recognised that water service provision can be inefficient when too many independent providers are involved. Hence, there is a growing tendency in OECD countries for water systems to be managed by groupings of municipalities so as to organise supply at a larger scale. Other forms of consolidation have also been occurring: the Netherlands, for example, reduced the number of water boards from 210 in 1950 to 15 in 2002 (van Dijk and Schwartz, 2002). The degree of management autonomy of local water utilities also seems to be increasing (OECD, 1999b).

Many cities, particularly in the developing world, urgently need comprehensive reform of policies and institutions to stop water infrastructure deterioration, promote efficient and sustainable water use, and generate revenue for needed investments. These reforms will inevitably require increased cost recovery, improved resource conservation, and more pollution prevention at the source.

Private sector participation

Since the mid-1990s, an important approach that has been gradually introduced in the water sector is the notion of partnerships between public and private agents. While the 1990s saw a significant increase in private sector participation in the water sector worldwide (Figure 5.2), it is still estimated that less than 10% of the world's population is provided with drinking water through private operators (Blokland, 2000). According to the World Bank, private sector participation is most common in Latin America, followed by

Figure 5.2.   **Number of projects with private participation (1990-2000)**

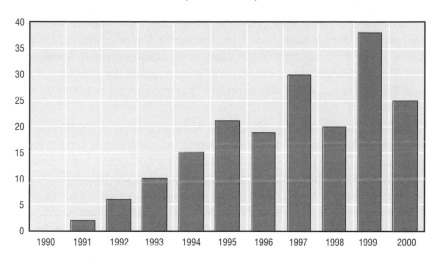

Source: OECD-World Bank (2002).

East Asia, Central Asia, and Eastern Europe. While the nature of private sector participation may range from partial financing of investments to an increasing role in the operation of services, most countries have opted for the concession approach, in which the private sector participates in managing some services but the public sector retains ownership of the system.

It is important to bear in mind that many examples of efficiently managed public water and sanitation utilities exist, and that the characteristics of the public sector differ among countries. Thus, in many countries, it is not necessarily the public sector *per se*, but factors such as faulty incentive structures, the politicisation of appointments and management, and other bureaucratic weaknesses that contribute to poor performance. Despite widespread belief in the potential for efficient use of the private sector in some areas of service provision, empirical evidence of the relative merits of private and public management in the water sector is relatively limited.

The most commonly cited advantages of private sector participation are that it brings technical and managerial expertise to the sector, improves operating efficiency, entails injections of capital and greater efficiency in its use, reduces the need for subsidies, and increases responsiveness to consumer needs and preferences. The private sector has significantly better access than governments to capital flows and to the technical know-how that will make a real difference in the provision of critical water services.

OECD experience suggests that while the commercialisation or involvement of the private sector in selected water supply services can work well, governments must assure vigilance for the public interest. Private participation in the delivery of urban water and sanitation services therefore requires more, rather than less, effective public intervention. Since many aspects of the water sector are not likely to be truly competitive due to the technological characteristics of service provision, public authorities will have to regulate the sector effectively to ensure that services are not overpriced (or under-provided).

Recent experience with private sector participation in non-OECD countries also suggests that there are major obstacles that significantly hinder greater involvement of the private sector on the provision of urban water services. Despite high hopes that private sector participation might help overcome the financing gap for achieving international goals for access to water and sanitation, an increasing number of water sector projects with private sector participation appear to be in crisis, often due to the difficult economic situation in the host country. The number of such projects has been decreasing in three out of the last five years for which data is available (Figure 5.2), and investment flows have been slowing over the last four years (OECD-World Bank, 2002). This has triggered recognition by both public and private actors of a number of systemic problems in the design of projects, for which solutions need to be found. These include weak regulatory set-ups in the host country, the lack of political support for private sector participation, the need for long-term debt finance, low returns on investment, fragmented deal size, poor credit-worthiness of local governments, poor contract and project structuring, and a frequently inappropriate allocation of risks between involved parties.

The following paragraphs outline some of the key lessons from OECD experiences with private sector investment in urban water and wastewater services (OECD, 2000).

- *If a government decides to involve private firms in meeting its responsibility, it also needs to shift from being the manager of the water system to being its overseer and regulator.*

As the provider of water services, the government manages all aspects of the water system. It decides what is to be built, who is to be hired to do what, how much is to be charged, what quality of water is to be provided, and all related matters. The government takes on a very different role if it decides to involve the private sector. At least for those tasks assigned to private business, the government stops being the day-to-day manager and becomes the overseer of the work. Making this shift is very difficult for many governments. The government's regulatory capacity becomes a critical consideration for potential private investors. If this capacity is weak, little international private capital will flow into the sector.

Governments have to remain involved in providing water services, even with private investment. The question for potential private investors is whether the form of the government's continued participation makes the investment more or less attractive than other opportunities. Much of the answer will depend on the clarity and predictability of the government's oversight.

● *Water fees are often too low to support major private investments.*

Many governments sell drinking water for prices well below the cost of providing the service. In some cases, this is to ensure that the basic needs of all citizens are met, even those who find it hard to pay. In other cases, it is to build political popularity or avoid the civil unrest that might accompany efforts to increase prices. For sanitation services and raw water abstraction, the prices are usually even lower. In each case, it is the political, not the economic, value of the water that often drives the calculation. The impact on potential private investors is clear – the lower the revenue stream, the smaller the investment they will be willing to make.

● *Water users are willing and able to pay for many water services.*

Since access to drinking water is a basic need, it has great value to individuals. Most urban dwellers already pay something for their drinking water, either through connections to formal, networked systems or via purchases from informal vendors and community-based providers. As a result, the potential revenue streams are sufficient to interest private investors in drinking water services over the long term. Even poorer, non-networked urban neighbourhoods can be viewed as reliable sources of revenue, given that they often pay more for their drinking water than wealthier areas do. More difficult issues arise for other parts of the water cycle, particularly wastewater collection and treatment. While people are often willing to pay to have sanitary wastes removed from their residences, they often value this service lower than access to clean drinking water. Even less consumer value is typically placed on treating sanitary wastes once they are taken away.

● *Addressing the social aspect of water provision is crucial for the success of private sector participation.*

Ensuring that all citizens have access to clean water, regardless of their ability to pay, is a key goal for most governments and an important prerequisite for the success of private sector participation. In many cases, insufficient measures to protect the poor have led to the loss of social acceptance of private participation, and thus to the collapse of the underlying project. If governments wish to subsidise the costs of water for the poor, they should do so in a way that supports income levels, rather than applying universally lower fees for water use. If water rates need to rise as part of moves to improve water services, public funds can help ease the transition. Governments can also provide retirement, relocation, or retraining support for employees affected by the shift to private investment. These types of public support – of limited duration and in gradually declining amounts – can promote the transition to a more efficient water sector over the long-term.

- ● *Costs and risks are often too high.*

High capital costs and low revenue streams are just two of the risks investors keep in mind when considering their options. Other major areas of concern include high up-front transaction costs, project-specific risks, and country-specific risks. If these costs and risks are perceived as too high, private operators will be reluctant to invest; in many developing countries, private business will opt in such cases for lower-risk forms of participation, such as management or lease contracts. Such options leave the responsibility for financing of investments with the public sector.

- ● *Governments and users are often not willing or ready to address risks to investors' satisfaction.*

Clearly, private investors must take responsibility for many risks – especially for the business risks that they are in the best position to manage, such as construction costs, treatment plant performance, and the efficiency of billing and collection. However, other risks are more properly assigned to governments or users. How each group deals with its responsibilities in such areas will have implications for the willingness of private firms to invest in particular infrastructure projects, and under which terms.

- ● *Private water operating companies are limited in number and cannot do everything.*

Since most governments wish to attract increased technical and managerial experience as well as potentially large sums of new private capital, the main focus of efforts to increase private sector participation has so far been on large international water companies. These firms tend to be viewed as "one-stop shops" for meeting all investment needs of the future system. While this approach can work well, it restricts the potential scope of private investment. International water companies do not have an unlimited capacity for investments. They will seek out and concentrate on the largest, most potentially profitable opportunities – typically municipalities of more than 500 000 people. Hence, investments in poorer or smaller service areas are often left out or delayed. New ways need to be found to involve more private investors – of various sizes, nationalities, and experience – in improving water services.

- *Municipalities need to set infrastructure performance standards to reflect local needs and demand.*

Customers of monopoly suppliers of drinking water rely on governments to control water quality, quantity, and price. Similarly, environmental advocates and raw water users look to governments to set and enforce standards for pollutant discharges to surface- and groundwater. The levels at which any of these standards are set will have major cost implications. Performance standards should strike a delicate balance between the need to protect customers and the environment and the need to maintain water services at an affordable level.

- *Local and central governments need to improve their regulatory capacity.*

The changing role of government in the water service sector implies a need for municipal officials to take on complicated new tasks, such as negotiating contracts with international water companies, regulating the private delivery of water services, and participating in financing for water projects. Governments need to help the officials make this transition. Possible strategies could include inter-municipal talent pools, reliance on professional advisers, and support from international financial institutions.

- *Choose the form of private involvement that best fits local needs.*

Many forms of private involvement are possible. There is no universal "right answer" on how to use private investment to help improve water services. Ultimately, governments need to devise arrangements that fit the local context, and some may decide that public-only is best. In such cases, measures (*e.g.* personnel incentives) may be needed to ensure efficiency reforms are implemented in the public sector. Where the private sector is hesitant to engage, it might be suitable to start with methods that involve low risk for the private operator (*e.g.* service contracts), moving only later towards more ambitious forms of involvement if considered appropriate.

- *Public awareness needs to be increased.*

Users will be willing to pay more for water services only if they understand the benefits they will receive. Providing users with information on options, product quality, and costs is therefore vital.

PART IV

Harnessing Science and Technology

Introduction

Ｎew technologies and scientific progress offer considerable scope for increasing the efficiency of water use and reducing water pollution. In the area of water use efficiency, many OECD countries have seen significant improvements in reducing leakage during the transfer of water and in the development of technologies to support lower water consumption. For example, improvements and investments in water transfer systems (pipes, etc.) in use have reduced water leakage rates from municipal systems to as low as 10-12% in some countries (OECD, 1998b). The installation and use of individual water meters, common for single-family residences in many OECD countries, has enabled volumetric water charging, which provides incentives to minimise water use.

Other technologies to help minimise use include low-water-use washing machines and dishwashers, timed garden sprinkler systems, and low-flush toilets in households; systems for water recycling or reuse as well as in-plant water treatment systems in industry; and drip irrigation systems or crop- and time-specific irrigation in agriculture. A related development is seawater desalinisation, which is providing an increasingly cost competitive source of additional water supply.

As concerns wastewater treatment, increased on-site treatment by large industrial water users is helping reduce the amounts of wastewater sent to municipal treatment facilities and of effluents released back into freshwater systems. A large majority of households in OECD countries are now connected to public or independent sewage treatment systems, which increasingly use not just primary or secondary processes but also tertiary treatment (i.e. advanced chemical treatment). However, the economic limit in terms of sewerage connection has been reached in some locations, so alternatives will need to be found for servicing small, isolated communities whose connection to the main sewerage system is not economically feasible.

One area in which the OECD has undertaken specific work is in efforts to improve drinking water purification systems. Its is of particular concern due to the number of illnesses and deaths attributed to contaminated drinking water and the vulnerability of water systems to outbreaks of waterborne diseases. The international community recommended international co-operation to improve assessment and management of the world's sources of drinking water at the 1996 OECD Workshop on Biotechnology for Water Use and Conservation (Cocoyoc, Mexico). In 1998, the OECD Interlaken Workshop on Molecular Technologies for Safe Drinking Water confirmed the need to examine the role and usefulness of the traditional parameters for monitoring drinking water, and called for better understanding of what information and management resources are needed for a systematic, preventive approach to the control of drinking water quality, from catchment to consumer. Responding to these requests, an expert group was formed to develop a joint WHO-OECD guidance document on improving the microbiological safety of drinking water (OECD-WHO, 2003). Chapter 6 draws on the results of this work.

ISBN 92-64-09948-4
Improving Water Management
Recent OECD Experience
© OECD 2003

Chapter 6

Technology and Information Needs for Improved Drinking Water Quality

Context

Inadequate drinking water supply, water quality, and sanitation are among the world's major causes of preventable morbidity and mortality. According to World Bank and WHO estimates, contaminated drinking water is responsible every year for some 5 million deaths, most of them in developing countries. Furthermore, half of all people in the developing world suffer from one or more of the six main diseases associated with poor water supply and sanitation (diarrhoea, ascaris, dracunculiasis, hookworm, schistosomiasis, and trachoma). Children are particularly at risk. Approximately 4 billion cases of diarrhoea per year cause 2 million deaths, mostly among children under age five.

The problem is not limited to developing countries. In OECD countries, outbreaks of waterborne diseases, particularly related to protozoan parasites, occur all too frequently and are a growing cause for concern. In the US in 1993, a major outbreak of gastrointestinal illness caused by the parasite *Cryptosporidium* was reported in Milwaukee, the largest city in Wisconsin. Some 400 000 residents were infected and more than 60 deaths were attributed to the outbreak (MacKenzie *et al.*, 1994; Craun *et al*, 2002). Cost estimates for this outbreak alone exceeded USD 54 million (MacKenzie *et al.*, 1994).

This dramatic event revealed the vulnerability of US water systems. It led in 1996 to a report, *Global Decline in Microbiological Safety of Water*, and a call for action by the American Academy for Microbiology. For OECD countries, the Milwaukee outbreak underscored the severe consequences of waterborne diseases. In spring 1994, a *Cryptosporidium* outbreak in Las Vegas, Nevada, further emphasised the urgency of reviewing the effectiveness and reliability of methods, management approaches, and technologies for guaranteeing the microbiological safety of drinking water. It indicated a need to re-evaluate what information is required to monitor and respond to adverse events. In addition, since the outbreak occurred in water that met guidelines for traditional indicators of microbial contamination, it called into question the effectiveness of such indicators as a basis for risk management.

More recent outbreaks have involved *E. coli* O157:H7. The most serious occurred in Spring 2000 in Walkerton, Ontario (Canada); it resulted in over 2 300 cases of infection and six deaths (Bruce-Grey-Owen Sound Health Unit, 2000). The number of outbreaks reported in the last decade demonstrates that transmission of pathogens by drinking water remains a significant problem worldwide. Despite substantial advances in recent years, access to safe drinking water is still a major public health challenge. Contributing factors include the discharge of greater quantities of wastewater, the ageing of water treatment infrastructure, and the increasing occurrence, or perhaps the increasing recognition and detection, of organisms resistant to conventional disinfection.

Meeting new challenges for drinking water quality

Assessment of the microbial quality of drinking water is currently based largely on culture techniques. These do not detect specific waterborne pathogens but rely on the monitoring of indicator bacteria (coliforms and enterococci), which reveal the potential presence of microbial pathogens of faecal origin.

The use of bacteria as indicators has proved successful in preventing the spread of waterborne cholera and typhoid, and is clearly suitable for protecting against bacterial pathogens such as salmonella and shigella. But it is not reliable for detecting viruses and protozoa: outbreaks attributed to such organisms have occurred when conventional testing has given no indication that water quality had been compromised (Barrell et al., 2000).

Moreover, traditional means of assessing microbial water quality are most commonly used for end-product monitoring, i.e. for testing drinking water as it leaves the treatment works and at the tap. The traditional indicators were originally developed for natural waters and are less suited for monitoring water after disinfection. Furthermore, end-product testing comes too late. When problems occur, and particularly in emergencies, it is necessary to take rapid decisions about the water supply system and public health and regulatory intervention. Unless sampling and measurement times are shorter than treatment or transit times, the contaminated water will have entered the distribution system or, worse, will have been consumed before the assessment has been completed.

Most of the outbreaks mentioned here were associated with contaminated drinking water. The most common cause of outbreaks involving community water supplies[1] has been contamination of the distribution system via cross-connections, back-siphonage, corrosion, or construction/repairs of the distribution system (Table 6.1). Others were due to inadequate treatment or undetermined causes.

In non-community systems, the large majority of outbreaks have been due to consumption of untreated or inadequately treated groundwater, with a few attributed to distribution deficiencies or undetermined causes.

From 1980 to 1999, 116 outbreaks of waterborne diseases were reported in Sweden. They affected about 58 000 people, and two deaths were reported

Table 6.1.   **Waterborne outbreaks and deficiencies in public water systems, US (1991-1998)**

Type of contamination	Community systems		Non-community systems	
	Outbreaks	Percentage	Outbreaks	Percentage
Surface water				
Untreated surface water	0	0	0	0
Inadequate or interrupted disinfection	4	18	1	50
Inadequate or interrupted filtration	4	18	0	0
Distribution system contamination	9	41	0	0
Inadequate control of chemical feed	2	9	0	0
Miscellaneous/unknown	3	14	1	50
Total surface water	22	100	2	100
Groundwater				
Untreated groundwater	5	23	18	35
Inadequate or interrupted disinfection	3	14	21	40
Inadequate or interrupted filtration	1	4	0	0
Distribution system contamination	8	36	8	15
Inadequate control of chemical feed	3	14	0	0
Miscellaneous/unknown	2	9	5	10
Total groundwater	22	100.0	52	100.0

Source: OECD (2001e).

(OECD, 2001e; Stanwell-Smith *et al.*, 2003). The most commonly identified organism involved was *Campylobacter*. About 70% of the outbreaks, however, were due to unknown agents causing acute gastrointestinal illness. The majority of these waterborne epidemics were most likely associated with undisinfected groundwater.

Between 1991 and 2000, 41 outbreaks were reported in the UK, with more than 3 768 reported cases of illness (OECD, 2001e; Stanwell-Smith *et al.*, 2003). Most of the outbreaks were due to *Cryptosporidium* and *Campylobacter*. The former is an emerging pathogen, and many water supply systems were/are not designed to cope with it. Most of the outbreaks of waterborne cryptosporidiosis occurred in situations where treatment integrity had been compromised or the treatment provided may have been inadequate. Untreated or inadequately filtered groundwater accounted for seven cases.

Further analysis of the US data indicates that although coliforms were found during the investigation of 46% of community and 83% of non-community system outbreaks, surveillance records showed that only 22% of the community and 9% of the non-community systems that experienced outbreaks had violated the national standard for coliform limits in the 12 months before the outbreak.

Thus, while traditional microbial parameters have proved useful and still have an important role to play, they may not provide a good indication of the potential for an outbreak. Monitoring of various aspects of the supply chain as well as of possible health effects requires different techniques, parameters, and approaches, and, above all, an integrated management method that takes the local context and needs into account.

Towards a total system approach for improved drinking water quality

The WHO-OECD guidance document (OECD-WHO, 2003) seeks to identify the key components of such an integrated approach. It moves away from using monitoring simply as a tool to verify the safety (or otherwise) of the finished product and towards using it as a basis for risk management decisions at every point in the system. Thus, it gives guidance on selecting and using various parameters and technologies to meet specific information needs and to support safe practice throughout the water system: catchment protection and assessment, assessment of source-water quality and of treatment efficiency, and monitoring of drinking water quality at the point of leaving the treatment facility and throughout the distribution system.

The guidance document reviews traditional index and indicator organisms as well as emerging technologies. It draws attention to important challenges relating to the preservation and management of safe drinking water and particularly to the need to develop a system that warns of the imminence of a hazardous situation and enables timely and cost-effective response. Emerging molecular methods are likely to make a significant contribution, as they offer the best hope for improved and rapid detection of microbial contaminants in water (Box 6.1).

The guidance document, which provides important background for the development of the third edition of the WHO Guidelines for Drinking Water Quality, supports a rapidly emerging approach to a broader, integrated perspective based on a risk management framework. It moves from the traditional indicator concept to propose multiple barriers and control of each treatment step so as to prevent contaminants from reaching the consumer. Consideration is also given to tolerable risk, water-quality targets, public health status, and education. This approach implies not only the integration of multiple parameters, but also a more encompassing or total system approach. Risk management is thus not confined to a single organisation or agency; national, regional, and local governments, water authorities, water supply agencies, and public health authorities all play a role. Since each of

Box 6.1. **Molecular techniques**

Novel molecular techniques often significantly increase the chances of detecting a pathogen from an implicated source of drinking water, particularly in the case of viruses with no readily available or rapid method of culture. These include rotaviruses, astroviruses, caliciviruses, hepatitis A virus, Norovirus (previously Norwalk-like virus), and other small round viruses (West, 1991). Traditional methods for detecting viruses are based on tissue-culture techniques that can take several weeks. While direct polymerase chain reaction (PCR) methods are faster, they are less sensitive than culture techniques when levels of viral particles are low. Combined tissue culture and PCR methods maximise the detection of viruses and reduce the time needed to a few days. New developments in PCR technology may eventually provide faster, more sensitive detection and quantification of viral particles.

Alternative methods for identifying/detecting potentially pathogenic bacteria include the use of in situ hybridisation and species-specific probes (Prescott and Fricker, 1999). These techniques make it possible to detect organisms within a few hours and can be adapted for use with any organism. On the horizon are also methods based on micro-arrays and biosensors. In the medical sector, biosensors have largely been based on antibody technology, with an antigen triggering a transducer or linking to an enzyme amplification system. Biosensors based on gene recognition may be very promising, particularly if coupled with the micro-array technology, since the latter makes it possible to process together several different probes targeting many different pathogens. This advantage could be invaluable for sample analysis during outbreaks.

these stakeholders has specific responsibilities and information needs, co-ordination and production of useful and compatible data are also major challenges.

Developing an integrated system of health and technical data

As mentioned above, the development of compatible data systems, particularly of health and technical data could contribute substantially to drinking water risk management. There are two main sources of data on the risks to health from drinking water: i) surveillance systems and other health studies, which produce epidemiological data; and ii) water quality monitoring by the water utility. The advantages and disadvantages of these sources differ in terms of assessing risk.

Water industry information can be classified under three main headings: i) regulatory monitoring (to comply with statutory standards of water quality); ii) process/operational monitoring (sampling to enable a water company to manage water treatment and distribution); and iii) research and development (*e.g.* developing new analytical tools or monitoring novel water treatment processes). Water industry data are comprehensive and complex but under-utilised, especially by the public health community. The epidemiological data, in contrast, are relatively heterogeneous, reactive, and limited in their risk identification potential (Table 6.2).

Table 6.2.   **Issues that might affect efficient use of water and health data**

Water data	Health data
Comprehensiveness varies by country	Not standardised
Usually geared towards statutory reporting	Need to maintain flexible methodological approach
Under-utilised	Frequently reactive
Not easily accessible to public health community	Lack of geographical resolution
Commercial sensitivity	Incomplete
Might under-estimate health risks	Not timely
Much data may not be timely	Potentially subject to significant bias

Source: OECD (2001e).

Ideally, a community would be best served by an integrated system of health and technical data, available as nearly as possible in "real time", which could be used for evidence-based risk assessment and active case searching.

EPISYS, an experimental system being used in north-eastern England in a collaboration between the health sector and the water industry (North of Tyne Communicable Disease Control Unit and Northumbrian Water Limited), might serve as a model. The project uses technical data and health care outcome data. The aim is to obtain real-time, geographically correlated health data, with multiple inputs and sophisticated mathematical analysis that can be correlated with technical data. The system aims to be:

● Person- or symptom-based.

● Sensitive.

● Timely.

● Usable as a baseline for future reference.

● Geared to community level.

● Amenable to rapid response.

So far, the system has been found to detect traditional episodes (salmonella in school children), track non-notifiable illnesses (viral community outbreaks), and detect episodes for which there is otherwise no data (viral illness, data from multiple sources). Further developments might include incorporation of environmental and geographical data sources and elaboration of predictive models.

The future

In coming decades, OECD countries will require significant effort and capital expenditure to meet demand for safe drinking water. More emphasis is needed on an integrated management approach, on R&D, and on education. Information on available good practice and technological solutions needs to be disseminated to potential users, and R&D on new technology should be encouraged. In view of the number of stakeholders involved and the increasing fragmentation of responsibility for drinking water supply and quality and for wastewater treatment, it will be essential to improve the integration of regulatory approaches and the compatibility of methods for monitoring and data collection.

Note

1. In the US, public water systems are classified as either "community" or "non-community". A "community" water system serves year-round residents of a community, subdivision or mobile home park with 15 or more service connections or an average of 25 or more residents. A "non-community" water system is used by the general public for 60 or more days a year and has at least 15 service connections or an average of 25 or more residents. Of the country's approximately 170 000 public water systems, 32% are "community" systems and 68% are "non-community" systems.

PART V

Working in Partnership with Developing Countries

Introduction

As Chapter 4 illustrates, a key challenge in transition economies is to ensure that adequate funds are available to maintain existing water service infrastructure and to extend services as needed to new households. The lack of financing for the management, operation, and maintenance of many water supply and treatment facilities ensures that they seldom run at reach full efficiency and thus deteriorate too rapidly, so that rehabilitation costs are higher than would otherwise be the case.

In less developed countries, especially those undergoing rapid urbanisation, a major challenge is to develop the most basic infrastructure to provide water services. Developing countries' opportunities for financing the provision of basic water services internally (*e.g.* through water charges and government support) is limited. Support from more developed countries is needed, in the form of ODA, foreign direct investment, capacity building, and technology transfers. Chapter 7 describes current trends in bilateral and multilateral ODA related to development of water supply and sanitation systems.

ISBN 92-64-09948-4
Improving Water Management
Recent OECD Experience
© OECD 2003

Chapter 7

Aid to the Water Supply and Sanitation Sector

Context

The OECD Development Assistance Committee (DAC) defines aid to water supply and sanitation as being that related to water resource policy, planning and programmes; water legislation and management, water resource development and protection; water supply and use; sanitation (including solid waste management); and education and training in water supply and sanitation. The definition excludes dams and reservoirs that are primarily for irrigation and hydropower, as well as activities related to river transport (these are classed under aid to agriculture, energy, and transport, respectively).

The DAC data relate to activities that have water supply and sanitation as their main purpose (Box 7.1). This implies some approximation, as the data fail to capture aid to the water sector extended within multi-sector programmes (e.g. integrated rural or urban development or general environmental conservation). Aid to the water sector delivered through non-governmental organisations may also be excluded, since this is not always sector coded in as much detail as project and programme aid.

The data cover both bilateral and multilateral aid to water supply and sanitation. For DAC countries, data on total aid commitments to the water sector are available from 1973 on. Detailed analysis is possible for the 1990s.[1] Data for the multilateral organisations cover commitments by the World Bank, the regional development banks, the International Fund for Agricultural Development, the European Development Fund, and, since 2000, UNICEF and UNDP.

Figure 7.1 illustrates the evolution in bilateral and multilateral financing of water projects in developing countries since 1973. The data (in constant dollars) show that DAC members' bilateral aid for the water sector increased over the first two decades at an annual average rate of 9%. The downward trend observed since the middle of the 1990s reflects cuts in Official Development Assistance (ODA) in general, though aid for water started decreasing later than that for other sectors. The share of aid for water supply and sanitation in total ODA remained relatively stable in the 1990s at 6% of bilateral and 4-5% of multilateral ODA. In recent years, total aid allocations to the water sector have averaged about USD 3 billion a year. An additional USD 1-1.5 billion a year is allocated to the water sector in the form of non-concessional lending (mainly by the World Bank).

Box 7.1. **Reporting on the purpose of aid in DAC statistics**

The DAC collects data on aid flows through two reporting systems: the annual aggregate DAC statistics and the activity-specific Creditor Reporting System (CRS). The former provide an overall picture of the geographical or purpose distribution of aid and of the relative importance of each recipient country, region, or purpose in the total. The CRS permits examination of the geographical and purpose breakdown simultaneously. Both systems collect the data in a standard electronic format and make them available on line and on CD-ROM (see *www.oecd.org/dac/stats*).

Reporting on the purpose of aid entails classification by sector and by policy objective. The sector code identifies "the specific area of the recipient's economic or social structure which the transfer is intended to foster". In DAC reporting (as in most donors' internal reporting systems), each activity can be assigned only one sector code. For activities cutting across several sectors, either a multi-sector code or the code corresponding to the largest component of the activity is used. This is not likely to impart a systematic bias to analyses of trends and orders of magnitude. The data may differ slightly from those provided by internal systems that allow a commitment to be assigned to more than one sector. However, at present the DAC system of a single sector code is the only practical method of standardising reporting on a basis that permits valid donor comparisons.

The sectoral data are supplemented by information on the policy objectives of aid: environmental sustainability, gender equality, reduction of poverty, and participatory development/good governance. Reporting is based on a marking system with three values: "principal objective", "significant objective", and "not targeted to the policy objective". Each activity can have more than one policy objective. The marker data are descriptive rather than quantitative.

Data on the purpose of aid are collected on commitments rather than disbursements. Using average data evens out the "lumpiness" of commitments and thereby increases the statistical significance of the data analysis. Moving averages give a clearer view of the underlying trends.

Table 7.1 presents data on aid for water supply and sanitation by individual donors. Japan is by far the largest donor in the sector in value terms, accounting for about one-third of total aid to water. Activities funded by the World Bank's International Development Association, Germany, the US, France, the UK, and the EC add up to a further 45%. The share of aid for water supply and sanitation in total sector-allocable ODA[2] is above the DAC average of 9% for Austria, Denmark, France, Germany, Japan and Luxembourg.

Figure 7.1. **Aid to water supply and sanitation commitments
(1973-2001; 5-year moving average)**
(constant 2000 prices)

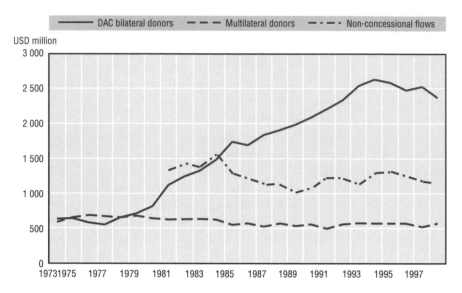

Source: OECD, DAC CRS.

Figure 7.2 breaks down aid for the water sector by subsector for the last five years. Water supply and sanitation projects account for over three-quarters of the contributions. Most of these projects have been classified under "large systems", but the number drawing on low-cost technologies (hand pumps, gravity-fed systems, rainwater collection, latrines, etc.) seems to be increasing.[3] The fact remains, though, that a handful of large projects undertaken in urban areas dominate aid for water supply and sanitation. Furthermore, many of these projects are financed through loans rather than grants. In 2000-01, for example, about 57% of total ODA in the water sector took the form of loans (over three-quarters of aid from Austria, France, Italy, Japan, Portugal and Spain was extended as loans). By comparison, the share of loans in ODA to all sectors combined in 2000-01 was 22%.

About 10% of aid in the water sector is directed to water resource policy, planning, and programmes. This category includes a few large programmes and reforms, and numerous smaller activities to improve water resource management through institutional support, technical assistance, and capacity building. Education and training in the water sector represents a tiny share of the total. It should be noted, however, that the data do not include education and training components of water supply and sanitation projects, which can rarely be separately identified.

Table 7.1. **Aid to water supply and sanitation by donor**

(1996-2001, annual average commitment and share in total sector-allocable aid)

	USD million		% of donor total		% All donors	
	1996-1998	1999-2001	1996-1998	1999-2001	1996-1998	1999-2001
Australia	23	40	3	6	1	1
Austria	34	46	17	18	1	2
Belgium	12	13	4	4	0	0
Canada	23	22	4	4	1	1
Denmark	103	73	15	13	3	2
Finland	18	12	11	8	1	0
France	259	148	13	13	7	5
Germany	435	318	19	11	13	11
Ireland	6	7	7	7	0	0
Italy	35	29	14	9	1	1
Japan	1 442	999	14	14	41	33
Luxembourg	2	8	4	13	0	0
Netherlands	103	75	8	7	3	2
New Zealand	1	1	2	2	0	0
Norway	16	32	4	5	0	1
Portugal	0	5	1	3	0	0
Spain	23	60	4	8	1	2
Sweden	43	35	6	6	1	1
Switzerland	25	25	7	6	1	1
United Kingdom[1]	116	165	8	7	3	5
United States	186	252	6	4	5	8
Total DAC	**2 906**	**2 368**	**11**	**9**	**83**	**78**
AfDF	56	64	10	9	2	2
AsDF	150	88	11	8	4	3
EC	..	216	..	5	..	5
IDA	323	331	6	6	9	11
IDB Sp F	46	32	9	9	1	1
Total Multilateral	**575**	**730**	**7**	**6**	**17**	**22**
Total	**3 482**	**3 098**	**10**	**8**	**100**	**100**

1. A DFID study shows that since 1999 actual expenditure for water supply and sanitation is about double the levels reflected here. Approximately half of the UK water expenditure takes place within multisector projects.
Source: OECD, DAC CRS.

Figure 7.2. **Water supply and sanitation aid commitments by subsector (1997-2001)**

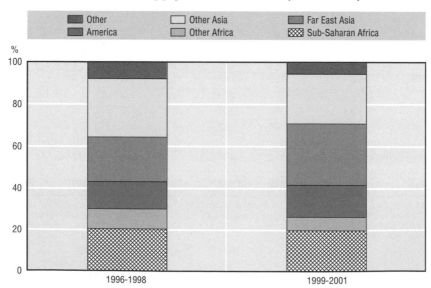

Source: OECD, DAC CRS.

Figure 7.3 shows aid in the water sector by region. About half of the total goes to Asia (roughly in line with Asia's share of total ODA commitments), with a focus on Far East Asia in recent years. The share of Africa has slightly decreased and that of America slightly increased.

Figure 7.3. **Geographical breakdown of aid commitments for water supply and sanitation (1996-2001)**

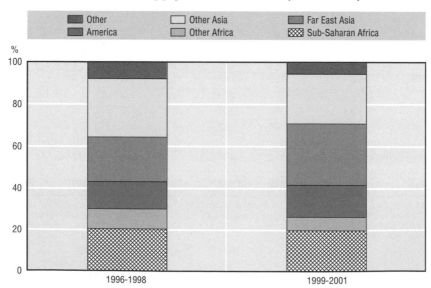

Source: OECD, DAC CRS.

Figure 7.4. **Aid for water supply and sanitation, by recipient – overview of targeting to countries most in need (2000-01)**

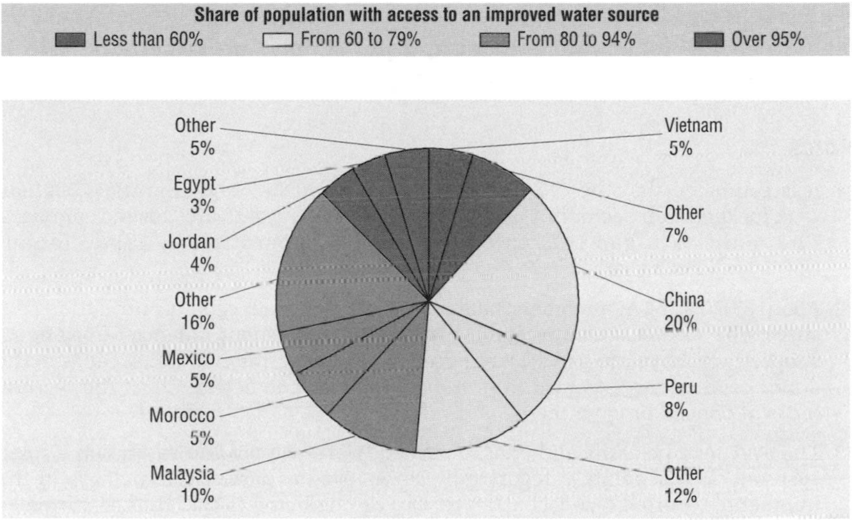

Share of population with access to an improved water source

■ Less than 60%　　□ From 60 to 79%　　▤ From 80 to 94%　　■ Over 95%

Source: OECD, DAC CRS; World Bank (2002).

Aid in the water sector is concentrated in a relatively few recipient countries (OECD, 1998e). In 1995-96, for example, ten countries received nearly two-thirds of aid in this sector. The data show some change in focus in recent years. In 1997-2001, the ten largest recipients received 48% of the total. China, India, Vietnam, Peru, Morocco, and Egypt were among the top ten in both periods, while Turkey, Indonesia, Tunisia, and Sri Lanka were replaced by Mexico, Malaysia, Jordan, and the Palestinian-administered areas.

The 1998 analysis also showed that many countries where a large proportion of the population lacked access to safe water received very little, if any, of the aid. As Figure 7.4 illustrates, this still seems to be the case. Only 12% of total aid to the water sector in 2000-01 went to countries where less than 60% of population has access to an improved water source,[4] which includes most of the least-developed countries.

Data on total aid for the water sector in a particular recipient country are not sufficient to permit analysis of whether aid is directed to where it is most needed. Projects in relatively rich countries may be targeted to the poorest regions or groups while projects in poor countries may tend to benefit the better off. The DAC "policy objective marker system" does, however, provide supplementary data that help in assessing features such as poverty and gender focus of aid activities.

Because of data quality limitations, generalised conclusions can be drawn only with caution; yet the data reported by 11 DAC members for 2000 and 2001 suggest that water projects are slightly less targeted on poverty and gender concerns than are projects in other sectors,[5] though gender issues do seem to be well taken into account in water supply and sanitation projects undertaken in rural areas.

Notes

1. It is estimated that the CRS database covers 85-90% of DAC countries' bilateral ODA for the water sector in 1990-95. From 1996 on, the data are close to complete. The main data gap relates to technical co-operation by Japan (about USD 80 million a year).

2. About 65-70% of DAC members' bilateral ODA is sector allocable. Contributions not susceptible to allocation by sector (*e.g.* structural adjustment, balance-of-payments support, actions relating to debt, emergency assistance, internal transactions in the donor country) are excluded from the denominator, to better reflect the sectoral focus of donors' programmes.

3. The DAC sector classification has identified "water supply and sanitation – small systems" as a separate category only since 1996, so part of the increase in the number of reported low-cost activities can be attributed to this change. However, there has also been a decrease in average project size since 1996. For 1995-96, of a total of 900 water supply and sanitation commitments, about 100 were for more than USD 10 million and accounted for 75% of the total value of aid to the sector for those two years. A similar analysis using 1999-2000 data (same donors) shows 75 out of a total of 1 400 projects at that funding level, or 60% of the total value.

4. This is the indicator used for monitoring progress towards the Millennium Development Goal of halving by 2015 the proportion of people without sustainable access to safe drinking water.

5. Australia, Canada (CIDA), Denmark, Finland, Germany (KfW), Japan, the Netherlands, Norway, Sweden, Switzerland, and the UK provide marker data for the majority of reported activities. Of the total number of water projects screened against the policy markers, less than half were reported as direct assistance to poor people (principal or significant objective) and one-fourth as targeting gender equality (the majority scoring significant objective). For comparison, about two-thirds of activities in the health sector had been reported as poverty-focused and one-third as targeting gender equality.

PART VI

Conclusions

Introduction

Over the last few decades, OECD countries have significantly reduced industrial point-source discharges to waterways, cleaned up some of their worst polluted surface waters, increased water use efficiency, and applied more integrated approaches to water basin management. Per capita water use has declined in most OECD countries, and 13 have even realised declines in total water use, despite rising incomes and populations. Almost 65% of the population in OECD countries is connected to public wastewater treatment plants, compared with 50% in 1980.

However, further efforts are still needed in some areas, including management of non-point sources of water pollution (*e.g.* agricultural and urban run-off), reducing pollution of groundwater resources, and applying efficient water pricing in agriculture. A major challenge is to assure the provision of sufficient water of high quality for human health, economic development, and ecosystem purposes.

Some of the main lessons that OECD countries have learned through their experiences with water management are presented below. Certain of these, based on the results of specific OECD projects, have been explored in more depth in this report. All together, the lessons fall into four areas: better use of market-based instruments (*e.g.* user charges, abstraction charges, tradable permits, removal of environmentally damaging subsidies); strengthened institutions for water management; development and dissemination of appropriate science and technology; and closer co-operation with non-OECD countries.

Making markets work

- *Assuring adequate financial resources*: Adequate funds are needed to assure the provision, maintenance, operation, expansion, and replacement of water supply and wastewater treatment infrastructure over time. Without such resources, water infrastructure will degrade, resulting in higher costs for maintenance and operation over the longer term, and reduced access to services. In some countries, such as certain EECCA countries, low collection rates for service charges exacerbate under-funding of water service provision and reduced efficiency in the pricing systems.

- *Charging at rates that reflect the full costs of water service provision:* Levying water charges that reflect the full costs of supplying the water services can help to: ensure that water ecosystems are adequated protected; ensure that adequate funds are available for the maintenance and expansion of water service infrastructure; reduce demands on limited public budgets to support water service provision; and provide incentives to individual water users to use water services efficiently. While many OECD countries are making progress towards reducing water subsidies, especially in the household and industrial sectors, subsidies remain common for agricultural water use. Meters to measure water use by individual users are needed so that water charges can reflect actual volumes used.

- *Addressing the negative social impacts of water pricing policies:* To promote access to affordable water supply and wastewater treatment services, a range of innovative mechanisms can be used to alleviate hardships caused by water pricing while still providing incentives for efficient water use. These include the increasing-block volumetric pricing structures (which charge increasing amounts per each additional unit of water used or wastewater treated) and the provision of rebates or reduced charges for groups such as low-income households, retired people, and single-parent families. Such measures are recommended in place of across-the-board subsidies that reduce prices (and, therefore, water conservation incentives) to all water users, not just those facing hardships.

Improving decision making

- *Applying integrated "whole-basin" and ecosystem approaches:* Increasingly, countries are recognising the benefits of managing water resources using a "whole-basin" or "river-basin" approach. This approach allows managers to balance water withdrawals and control water-polluting activities across the full basin, ensuring that upstream uses are consistent with downstream water quantity and quality requirements. Many water bodies cross local or national boundaries, and so do the associated challenges in managing their use and controlling pollution to them. Much progress has been made in the development of bilateral, regional, and multilateral agreements to manage such waters using an integrated whole-basin approach, although better implementation is needed. Ecosystem approaches to water management are also increasing, as are approaches which integrate nature conservation and water management policies.

- *Working with the private sector:* A general trend is apparent in OECD countries away from a fully public model of supply of water and sanitation services, and towards systems with partial or full ownership and/or management by municipal authorities, private sector operators, farmer associations, or

NGOs. In many cases, the systems remain publicly owned, but responsibility for their management is delegated to private operators via concessions. Governments usually retain at least an oversight or regulatory role, to assure efficient, equitable, and affordable access to high-quality services. Under certain circumstances, public-private partnerships can bring increased technical and managerial expertise and capital investments, along with reduced subsidies.

Harnessing science and technology

- *Improved technologies for protecting drinking water quality:* The majority of water-related illnesses and deaths occur in developing countries, yet drinking water systems in OECD countries are not immune to waterborne disease outbreaks. OECD countries have been reviewing the effectiveness and reliability of management approaches and technologies intended to guarantee the microbiological safety of drinking water. Increased emphasis is being placed on an integrated management approach to drinking water provision, on more stringent drinking water quality standards and comprehensive microbial testing systems and data collection, and on new water purification technologies.

- *Improving the efficiency of water use.* Scientific and technological developments have significantly helped in reducing leakage from water transfer systems (pipes, etc.) and in increasing the technical efficiency of water use. Technologies include individual water meters, low-water-use household washing machines, dishwashers, and toilets, and crop- and time-specific irrigation. While many of these are highly effective, incentives (*e.g.* appropriate water price signals, regulations, and occasionally support for installation) are often needed to ensure that they are widely used. Meanwhile developments in areas such as desalinisation of seawater and reuse of wastewater are increasing the availability of cost-competitive additional supply.

Partnerships with developing countries

- *Supporting international water goals:* Bilateral and multilateral aid for the water supply and wastewater treatment sector increased at an average rate of 9% per year in recent decades, before declining from 1995 in line with the broader decrease in ODA. Aid flows and co-operation between OECD and developing countries on water supply and wastewater treatment need to increase significantly if the Millennium Development Goal on access to water and the World Summit on Sustainable Development (WSSD) target on access to wastewater treatment services are to be met.

OECD work on water management: what next?

The commitment by heads of state and government at WSSD to halve the proportion of people who do not have access to basic sanitation by 2015 complemented the earlier Millennium Development Goal to halve the proportion of people without access to safe drinking water. The WSSD Plan of Implementation goes even further, outlining specific actions to achieve the goal and to better manage water resources for human health, ecosystem needs, and economic development.

Among these actions are: mobilising international and domestic finances, technologies, and capacity building for water infrastructure and service development; intensifying water pollution prevention to reduce health hazards and protect ecosystems; using the full range of policy instruments for efficient water management while assuring affordable water services for all; and facilitating the establishment of public-private partnerships. Countries agreed to develop integrated water resource management and water efficiency plans by 2005 with regard to integrated river basin, watershed, and groundwater management. They agreed to work together to improve understanding of the water cycle, and to help support developing and transition economies in their efforts to monitor and assess water quality and quantity (paragraphs 24-28, WSSD Plan of Implementation).

These concrete actions for protecting and enhancing water resources worldwide strengthen previous intergovernmental commitments, including those made through the First and Second World Water Forums (1997 and 2000, respectively) and the Bonn International Conference on Freshwater (2001). It is expected that the Third World Water Forum (Japan, March 2003) will build on these commitments and actions as participants share practical experiences in the sustainable management of water resources.

Through the OECD and other forums, OECD member countries have been working together to further define the specific water-related challenges they face and the actions needed to tackle them. This work complements developments in the broader international arena. The *OECD Environmental Strategy for the First Decade of the 21st Century* (OECD, 2001d), which OECD Environment Ministers adopted in 2001, outlines five key objectives of environmental policy for OECD countries. The first is "maintaining the integrity of ecosystems through the efficient management of natural resources", with a particular focus on three priority issues:[1] climate, freshwater, and biodiversity.

The *OECD Environmental Strategy* identified two overarching challenges facing OECD countries in their management of freshwater, relating to both the quantity and quality of supplies: to manage freshwater resources and watersheds in such a way as to maintain adequate supplies both for human use and for environmental purposes; and to protect and, where necessary, restore water bodies so as to meet national and international water quality objectives.

To address these challenges, OECD countries agreed to take a range of national actions by 2010. These actions reflect internationally agreed targets and actions, particularly those outlined in the WSSD Plan of Implementation.[2] They include actions to assure: the quality of water sources, access by all to safe drinking water and sanitation, and application of the ecosystem approach to watershed management; more efficient and cost-effective use of available resources through the use of policies to recover the full costs of water provision (taking into account the social impacts of such policies) and to reduce leakage; and inclusion of the transboundary and public-good nature of water in management policies, focusing on the need to manage transboundary water systems co-operatively and to support capacity building and technology transfer that help developing countries in their management of freshwater resources.

As the OECD Environmental Strategy specifies, the OECD is continuing its work to support countries in the implementation of better water management policies. Areas of work under way or recently completed include: a comparison of the performance of OECD country water management systems, based on the results of their OECD Environmental Performance Reviews (OECD, 2003a); a study on the social aspects of water pricing systems and how and negative distributive effects of water charging can be alleviated (OECD, 2003b); and work on the use of domestic transferable permits for managing water use and controlling pollution (OECD, 2002c).

In addition to work undertaken in follow-up to the OECD Environmental Strategy, the OECD has a number of activities related to water management issues that support specific elements of the WSSD Plan of Implementation. These include participation in water-related WSSD Type II Partnership Initiatives. The first such initiative, for development of a Euro-Mediterranean Water and Poverty Facility, will bring together various partners to develop common strategies and action plans for addressing social and poverty concerns in the development of water projects and provision of water-related services. The OECD will apply the experiences gained through efforts in member countries to address the social aspects of water pricing, outlined in Chapter 3.

The second water-related WSSD Type II Partnership Initiative in which OECD will participate is the EU Water Initiative: Water for Life, in which the OECD will help develop strategies and tools for better management of urban water supply and sanitation systems in EECCA countries. This work will contribute to the development and implementation of a new East-West

Environmental Partnership, another Type II Initiative launched at the WSSD, which will be submitted to the Environment for Europe Ministerial Conference (Kiev, Ukraine, May 2003). The OECD contribution will draw on recent work in the region, including experiences with the use of the *FEASIBLE©* tool to help countries better plan the financing of urban water supply systems (see Chapter 4).

Other water-related OECD work focuses on areas in which the value added is specific to the OECD; that is, they reflect its nature as an intergovernmental, economics-based institution supporting countries in the development of sustainable and economically efficient policies and the monitoring of their implementation. Examples include work that:

- Develops better water management policies through individual country reviews (*i.e.* the water chapters of the OECD Environmental Performance Reviews and selected sustainable development sections of the OECD Economic Surveys) and the collection of data and indicators reflecting developments in water body quality, connection rates to various levels of sewerage treatment systems, water prices, and water use efficiency.

- Develops analysis, shares experiences, and provides analytical tools for enhancing the use of environmentally effective and economically efficient policy instruments to support better water management, as well as to address any negative distributive effects of such policy instruments.

- Promotes the development and dissemination of technological and scientific methods and systems that can help increase microbial drinking water quality and enhance the efficiency of water use and wastewater treatment.

- Supports OECD donor countries in the development of co-operative programmes with developing countries for the achievement of internally agreed targets on access to clean drinking water and adequate sanitation systems.

Through all this work, the OECD will continue to support strengthened government policies and regulatory systems for water management in an economically efficient, environmentally sound, and socially responsible manner.

Notes

1. The priority issues were identified through the *OECD Environmental Outlook* (OECD, 2001a), which identified recent and projected changes in environmental conditions and pressures for OECD countries to 2020.

2. See Box 2.1 in Chapter 2 for further details on the freshwater section of Objective 1 of the *OECD Environmental Strategy*.

References

Barrell, R.A.E., P.R. Hunter, and G. Nichols (2000),
"Microbiological standards for water and their relationship to health risk", *Communicable Disease and Public Health*, Vol. 3; No. 1, pp. 8-13.

Blokland, M. (2000),
"Water and Public-Private Partnerships", paper presented at the Second World Water Forum, 17-22 March 2000, The Hague, Netherlands.

Bruce-Grey-Owen Sound Health Unit (2000),
"The investigative report on the Walkerton outbreak of waterborne gastroenteritis", *http://water.sesep.drexel.edu/outbreaks/WalkertonReportOct2000/REPORT_Oct00.PDF*

Catley-Carlson, M. (1999),
"Some Considerations Relating to Population Growth and Water Supply and Sanitation", paper presented at the expert panel on institutions and implications on water resources, 18-19 February 1999, Paris.

Cosgrove, W.J. and F.R. Rijsberman (2000),
World Water Vision: Making Water Everybody's Business, Earthscan Publications for World Water Council, London.

Craun, G.F., R.L. Calderon, and N. Nwachuku (2002),
"Causes of Waterborne Outbreaks in the United States, 1991-1998", *Drinking Water and Infectious Disease: Establishing the Links*, P.R. Hunter et al. (eds.), CRC Press, London, pp. 105-117.

Van Dijk, M.P. and K. Schwartz (2002),
"Financing the Water Sector in the Netherlands: A First Analysis", paper presented at the Financing Water Infrastructure Panel in the Hague, 8 October 2002, Netherlands Water Partnership, Delft.

Johnstone, N. and L. Wood (2001),
Private Firms and Public Water: Realising Social And Environmental Objectives In Developing Countries, Edward Elgar Publishing, International Institute for Environment and Development, UK.

MacKenzie, W.R., N.J. Hoxie, M.E. Proctor, M.S. Gradus, K.A. Blair, D.E. Peterson, J.J. Kazmierczak, D.G. Addiss, K.R. Fox, J.B. Rose, and J.P. Davis (1994), "A massive outbreak in Milwaukee of *Cryptosporidium* infection transmitted through the public water supply", *New England Journal of Medicine*, Vol. 331, No. 3, pp. 161-167.

OECD (1998a),
Towards Sustainable Development: Environmental Indicators, OECD, Paris.

OECD (1998b),
Water Consumption and Sustainable Water Resources Management, OECD, Paris.

OECD (1998c),
Water Management: Performance and Challenges in OECD Countries, OECD, Paris.

OECD (1998d),
  Sustainable Management of Water in Agriculture: Issues and Policies, proceedings of Athens workshop, OECD, Paris.

OECD (1998e),
  Development Co-operation Report: Efforts and Policies of the Members of the Development Assistance Committee, OECD, Paris.

OECD (1999a),
  OECD Environmental Data: Compendium 1999, OECD, Paris.

OECD (1999b),
  The Price of Water: Trends in OECD Countries, OECD, Paris.

OECD (1999c),
  Household Water Pricing in OECD Countries, Paris.

OECD (2000),
  Global Trends in Urban Water Supply and Waste Water Financing and Management: Changing Roles for the Public and Private Sectors, OECD, Paris.

OECD (2001a),
  OECD Environmental Outlook, OECD, Paris.

OECD (2001b),
  Environmental Indicators for Agriculture Volume 3: Methods and Results, OECD, Paris. Executive Summary available at: *www.oecd.org/agr/env/indicators.htm* (see "Publications").

OECD (2001c),
  Sustainable Development: Critical Issues, OECD, Paris.

OECD (2001d),
  OECD Environmental Strategy for the First Decade of the 21st Century, OECD, Paris.

OECD (2001e),
  "Establishing Links between Drinking Water and Infectious Disease", Conclusions of the 2000 Expert Group Meeting, Basingstoke, UK, 9-11 July 2000, DSTI/STP/BIO(2001)12/FINAL, OECD, Paris.

OECD (2002a), *OECD Environmental Data: Compendium 2002*, OECD, Paris.

OECD (2002b),
  "Poverty-Environment Gender Linkages", *The DAC Journal 2001*, Vol. 2, No. 4, OECD, Paris. Also available at *www.oecd.org/pdf/M00034000/M00034776.pdf*

OECD (2002c),
  Implementing Domestic Tradable Permits: Recent Developments and Future Challenges, OECD, Paris.

OECD (1992-2002),
  OECD Environmental Performance Reviews, OECD, Paris.

OECD (2003a),
  OECD Environmental Performance Reviews – Water: Performance and Challenges in OECD Countries, OECD, Paris.

OECD (2003b),
  Social Issues in the Provision and Pricing of Water Services, OECD, Paris.

OECD (2003a forthcoming),
> *Guidelines for Consumer Protection and Public Participation in Urban Water Sector Reform in Eastern Europe, Caucasus and Central Asia*, OECD, Paris.

OECD (2003b forthcoming),
> *Background Analysis for the Financing Strategy for Wastewater Collection and Treatment in Selected Municipalities of the Sichuan Province, China*, OECD, Paris.

OECD-DANCEE (2001a),
> *Municipal Water Services, Kazakhstan – Background Analysis for the Financing Strategy*, OECD, Paris, and Danish Co-operation for Environment in Eastern Europe, Copenhagen.

OECD-DANCEE (2001b),
> *Municipal Water and Wastewater Sector in Georgia – Background Analysis for the Financing Strategy*, OECD, Paris, and Danish Co-operation for Environment in Eastern Europe, Copenhagen.

OECD-IWA (2001),
> *Water Management and Investment in the New Independent States*, proceedings of a consultation between economic/finance and environment ministers, Almaty, Kazakhstan, OECD, Paris, and International Water Association, London.

OECD-WHO (2003),
> *Assessing Microbial Safety of Drinking Waters: Perspectives for Improved Approaches and Methods*, OECD, Paris, and World Health Organization, Geneva.

OECD-World Bank (2002),
> *Private Sector Participation in Municipal Water Services in Central and Eastern Europe and Central Asia*, proceedings of a conference held 10-11 April 2002, Paris, OECD, and World Bank, Washington, DC.

Romanyuk, O. and V. Sapioglo (2002),
> "Are households willing to pay more for better services", results of effective demand modeling for communal services, PADCO and USAID, Kiev.

Prescott, A.M. and C.R. Fricker (1999),
> "Use of PNA oligonucleotides for the *in situ* detection of *Escherichia coli* in water", *Molecular and Cellular Probes*, Vol. 13, pp. 261-268.

Project Preparation Committee (2002),
> "Compilation of PPC Donor Profiles: A Survey of Donor Funding for Environmental Assistance to Central and Eastern Europe and the NIS", the Project Preparation Committee, June 2002.

SEI (Stockholm Environment Institute) (1997),
> *Comprehensive Assessment of the Freshwater Resources of the World*, Stockholm Environment Institute, Stockholm.

Stanwell-Smith, R., Y. Andersson and D.A. Levy (2003),
> "National Surveillance Systems", in *Drinking Water and Infectious Diseases: Establishing the Links*, P.R. Hunter, M. Waite and E. Ronchi (eds), CRC Press, London, pp. 25-40.

UN (United Nations) (2000),
> *United Nations Millennium Declaration*, 18 September 2000, UN, New York.

UNCSD (UN Commission on Sustainable Development) (1998),
> *Report of the Expert Group Meeting on Strategic Approaches to Freshwater Management*, UN, New York.

UNECE (UN Economic Commission for Europe) (2000),
Environmental Performance Review of Armenia, UNECE, Geneva.

UNEP (UN Environment Programme) (1997),
Global Environmental Outlook, United Nations Environment Programme, Nairobi.

UNEP (2000),
GEO 2000 Overview, UNEP, Nairobi.

UN WEHAB Working Group (2002),
"A Framework for Action on Water and Sanitation", presented at the World Summit on Sustainable Development, Johannesburg, South Africa.

West, P.A. (1991),
"Human pathogenic viruses and parasites: emerging pathogens in the water cycle", *Society for Applied Bacteriology Symposium Series*, Vol. 20, 107S-114S.

WHO-UNICEF (2000),
Global *Water Supply and Sanitation Assessment 2000 Report*, WHO, Geneva, and United Nations Children's Fund, New York.

World Bank (2002),
World Development Indicators 2002, World Bank, Washington, DC.

WRI (World Resources Institute),
UNEP, UNDP (United Nations Development Programme), and World Bank (1994),
World Resources 1994-95, Oxford University Press, New York.

WRI, UNEP, UNDP, and World Bank (1999),
World Resources 1998-99, Oxford University Press, New York.